CITYSPOTS

# VILNIU

Jeroen van Marle & Andrew Quested

£2.99
7/37

**Written by Jeroen van Marle and Andrew Quested**

Original photography by Andrew Quested and Richard Schofield
Front cover photography © Kevin Foy/Alamy Images
Series design based on an original concept by Studio 183 Limited

**Produced by Cambridge Publishing Management Ltd**
Project Editor: Tim Ryder
Layout: Trevor Double
Maps: PC Graphics
Transport map: © Communicarta Ltd

**Published by Thomas Cook Publishing**
A division of Thomas Cook Tour Operations Limited
Company Registration No. 1450464 England
PO Box 227, Unit 18, Coningsby Road
Peterborough PE3 8SB, United Kingdom
email: books@thomascook.com
www.thomascookpublishing.com
+ 44 (0) 1733 416477

ISBN-13: 978-184157-650-3
ISBN-10: 1-84157-650-6


Series/Project Editor: Kelly Anne Pipes
Production/DTP: Steven Collins

Printed and bound in Spain by GraphyCems

## CONTENTS

### INTRODUCING VILNIUS



### MAKING THE MOST OF VILNIUS



### THE CITY OF VILNIUS



### OUT OF TOWN



### PRACTICAL INFORMATION



### MAP LIST

## SYMBOLS & ABBREVIATIONS

The following symbols are used throughout this book:

address telephone fax email website address
opening times public transport connections important

The following symbols are used on the maps:

| | |
|---|---|
| information office | city |
| airport | large town |
| hospital | small town |
| police station | motorway |
| bus station | main road |
| railway station | minor road |
| metro | railway |
| cathedral | |

1 numbers denote featured cafés & restaurants

Hotels and restaurants are graded by approximate price as follows:
£ budget ££ mid-range £££ expensive

Strolling down Gedimino Prospektas towards the Cathedral

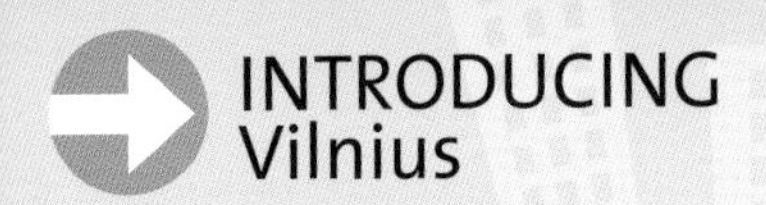
INTRODUCING
Vilnius

# Introduction

There's something about Vilnius that can capture you in a way that few other cities can.

There are, however, no clichés about Vilnius that capture it all. There is no main attraction – Vilnius just isn't like that. It doesn't conform to any expectations, wriggles free of the confines of any headline and refuses to be slotted into any particular category. It's not the best party town, it doesn't have the most striking post-Soviet architecture, the shopping is rubbish, it wouldn't make a good backdrop for a fairytale and it's not even the best example of Lithuanian culture (that honour goes to Kaunas, Lithuania's second-largest city). Hannibal Lecter might have been born in Vilnius, but he's a fictional character (and not a very nice one) and no one goes around wearing nail-jaw face masks – so that doesn't put Vilnius on the map either.

But while it refuses to grab headlines, Vilnius has an uncanny ability to capture hearts.

Backpackers huddle together in dorms and talk about the vibe, man, while those who prefer 5-star hotels will simply comment on the eclectic everything and thoroughly pleasant atmosphere.

There's an architectural and historical mishmash in Vilnius that is the sort of thing that can't be captured in a single image, but happily seeps into your senses over the duration of your visit and then refuses to leave when you do. No wonder so many people come back.

It is often said that you can stand anywhere in Vilnius, turn around, and see at least a few churches. More importantly, however, you will see a range of architectural styles that no other cities can match. Vilnius is the capital of what was once a regional superpower, and attracted many influences. It has also fallen victim to a variety of conquerors who have left their disparate dabs in various ways. Not only do you get a sense of all this from the crazy collection of styles nestled among a confusing array of cobbled streets, but you get a feeling that it's still happening. New buildings are going up all over the place while old ones are restored.

Now, Vilnius is a rapidly growing and gently bustling city with a strong student population and maturing service industries. You can see this in the streets every day. Fashion is flexible. People, ranging from the strutting and confident to the aimless amblers, can be themselves. There are the occasional 'local characters' – complete nutters mostly – who are tolerated and almost accepted as being a part of the character of the city.

They all contribute to a city that refuses to be classified, other than to say that it has a marvellous quirky charm – one that we can hint at but can never really capture, and one that we hope you will enjoy seeing for yourself during your stay in Vilnius.

*The Cathedral is one of Vilnius's major attractions*

# When to go

## CLIMATE

June and July are really the only months in which warm weather can be guaranteed, but, of course, are also the only times during which crowds of tourists can be counted upon to fill the tiny streets while many locals abandon the city for their holidays. Summer days are long, and many hours can be spent at pleasant outdoor cafés waiting for the late evening sunset. July also happens to be the month with the most rainfall, and you can find yourself running for cover from a sudden downpour.

Those who are inclined to worry more about the quality of the experience than the quality of the weather will enjoy a visit in spring or autumn – both of which offer explosions of colour, pleasant weather, fewer tourists, and the full bustle of a thriving city.

Winters are for the hardy. Temperatures occasionally drop below −20°C, and dirt, snow and mud become a feature of the 'warmer' days. The days themselves are depressingly short in mid-winter, with no more than eight hours of dim, cloud-choked light. No wonder tanning salons are popular.

The cold, however, does offer its own treats. Those who don't mind spending a little more time getting dressed, and then getting dressed again on top of whatever you just got dressed in – layer upon layer – can enjoy crunchy-snow walks in the park, activities such as ice-fishing and walking on frozen lakes, mucking about in the snow, or just listening to the constant warlike rumble of a flowing yet frozen river.

*A view of the Old Town skyline*

Being as flat as it is, Lithuania is not a downhill skiing destination. There *is* some skiing, but other than cross-country skiing it's of a rather pathetic variety that keeps locals mildly amused and expat adventure fans infernally frustrated: *There's all this snow, and nowhere to ski!* Don't come here for downhill skiing.

## ANNUAL EVENTS

Events are scattered throughout the year and, while they are certainly interesting, tend not to be the sort of highlights around which you will want to schedule your visit – unless you have some specific interest.

There tends to be a mix of pagan and Christian traditions when it comes to celebrations. You're as likely to see silly masks, decorations made from twigs and grass, and burning wicker people as you are to see crosses, religious robes and a nativity scene with a comically oversized baby Jesus. Things can get a bit Woodstock-Glastonbury at times, especially if you head out of town.

The pagan-Christian mix is also evident in the schedule of the events, with Christian calendar highlights such as Easter (*Velykos*) and Shrovetide (*Užgavėnės*) nestled among, or even married with, more pagan (nature-inspired) events such as the end of winter or midsummer. Add to this a few days to celebrate political and historical events, and you've got an interesting calendar, which is further bolstered by the fact that Vilnius sure knows how to celebrate. The city often erects a stage in the Cathedral Square for concerts and celebrations. They are, however, not very good at advance planning or promoting events to foreigners, so it can be hard to know what is happening until it is actually happening, or has just happened and someone tells you about what a great gig you just missed.

Some details and specific dates for concerts, performances, museum exhibitions and so forth are covered on the Entertainment Bank website www.eb.lt

### Shrovetide

If you happen to be in Vilnius on 28 February – or the weekend closest to it – you will see the celebration of Užgavėnės, otherwise known as Shrovetide or Pancake Day. The most enjoyable part of this is seeing the locals dressed up in silly costumes and masks. The masks in particular are impressive, and often delicately tread the line between cute and creepy. The characters represented include gypsies, travellers, doctors and nurses. Some people also dress up as

**PUBLIC HOLIDAYS**

**New Year's Day and National Flag Day** 1 January
**Independence Day** 16 February
**Restoration of Independence Day** 11 March
**Easter Sunday** 16 April
**A day off for the workers** 1 May
**Mother's Day** 7 May
**Day of Mourning and Hope** 14 June
**Joninės (Midsummer)** 24 June
**Crowning of Mindaugas** 6 July
**Žolinė (Feast of the Assumption)** 15 August
**Black Ribbon Day (Molotov-Ribbentropp)** 23 August
**Crowning of Vytautas the Great** 8 September
**Constitution Day** 25 October
**All Saints Day** 1 November
**Christmas Day** 25 December

storks, goats or horses. There will be mock fights between some of these characters, plenty of snowball throwing, singing and chanting – and it all culminates in the burning of a huge wicker woman. Most of the activities will take place in the Town Hall Square, although you could cop a snowball in the back of the head anywhere.

**Joninės (Midsummer), 23 June**

This is a good example of a pagan holiday that has taken on a Christian meaning. The national holiday, also known as Rasų, Cupola and Dew, celebrates the longest day and shortest night. The middle of summer has been identified as St John's Day, although there's actually nothing Christian about the way it is celebrated.

*Wearing a floral wreath for Joninės*

Traditionally, girls would braid wreaths from field grass and flowers and walk around looking like they have just been dragged upside-down through a meadow. In the current times of sexual equality, men are also welcome to put undergrowth on their heads.

At midnight, girls take off their wreaths and set them afloat in the river. Girls who are in relationships but are not yet married set two wreaths floating off together and believe that if they stay together, they will marry their loved one, whereas if the wreaths float apart, they will split up. There are also games of the 'he loves me, he loves me not' petal-pinching variety.

A huge fire is often lit close to midnight, and there are many rafts that are set alight and set floating down the river. Indeed, there will be all manner of flaming flotsam and jetsam bobbing down the river, so a spot on a bridge at midnight can be worth aiming for. The White Bridge (*Baltasis Tiltas*) is particularly popular for this purpose.

If you really want to get involved in the biggest Joninės celebration, head for the town of Kernavė, about 50 km west of Vilnius. Things tend to be very pagan here, and you'll feel like you've travelled back in time as hessian-clad hippies sing, dance, drink mead and set fire to things – all with birds' nests on their heads.

Kernavė is a village of great archaeological significance, and, in addition to hosting the biggest Joninės celebration, also hosts a **Live Archaeology Festival**, sometimes also called Days of Living History, where you can experience life pretty much as it would have been in ancient times. You can hack bits off a flame-grilled pig, sit in a tepee made of twigs, try archery and try not to get between the knights in shining armour bashing each other with sticks and maces. The festival normally takes place a couple of weeks after Joninės, in early July. See the Kernavė website for details ⓦ www.kernave.org

## Kaziukas Fair

While still dressed in pretty white snow, Vilnius explodes with colour on the first weekend in March as handy craft types flood in from all over the country to sell their wares at *Kaziukas Mugė* – St Casimir's Fair.

As is the case with many celebrations in Lithuania, however, the links to Christianity are mixed with something more like an updated version of an old pagan celebration of the end of winter.

St Casimir is the patron saint of Lithuania. While he died on 4 March, the roots of pagan celebrations held at this time of year had more to do with the appearance of crows. It's when, presumably, people emerged from their homely hibernation to trade the whittled wooden spoons, woven baskets and dried flower creations that they had been working on all winter. March would have been good for travelling and trading in the very old times as it was warm enough to go outside, and there was still enough snow to drag a sleigh over.

These days, on this weekend, a good portion of the city is given over to trading in the form of a market, although you don't see too many horses dragging sleighs any more. There's a bit of a floral theme to the weekend, with *verba* – sticks decorated with dried flowers and grasses from the previous summer – being sold just about everywhere, and being carried by almost everyone. You'll also have the opportunity to pick up hand-woven baskets, woodwork, whittled wooden spoons and other utensils, ironwork, ceramics, and all sorts of other things that don't come with bar codes.

In pagan tradition, *verba* had powers of life, health, disease prevention and making the house a bit less stinky. Houses would therefore be decorated with the colourful floral sticks, and people

would playfully strike each other on the shoulders and head with them. The *verba* of today range in size, and some are very big and thick, and therefore not really well-suited for such antics. After Christianity came to Lithuania, *verba* would also be carried to church on Palm Sunday (*Verbų Sekmadienis*), probably because they're arrestingly pretty, and there aren't too many palm trees in Lithuania.

Woodwork and basketwork are also popular, and some of the creations you will find on the many stalls are stunning. You can find yourself standing with your head tipped at an awkward angle wondering, 'what's that for?'

*Kaziukas* is not only interesting for the colour, hustle and bustle of the market, and the beautiful *verba* that seem to float above the heads of the crowd; there is also a nice feeling of celebration in the air as winter is coming to a close. It's also a good example of the mix of pagan and Christian traditions that are now so much a part of Lithuanian culture.

*Vilnius takes to the streets for the Kasiukas Fair*

# History

The region where Lithuania now lies was once covered by a glacier, and first occupied by reindeer when it receded. Hunting tribes were not far behind them, as early as the seventh century BC. Vilnius itself first came into being in the eleventh century, when a wooden castle was built on Gediminas' Hill to overlook a small settlement below.

It's been nothing but trouble since then. Lithuania has gone through many struggles, and at one point found itself to be a huge regional superpower, stretching as far southeast as the Black Sea.

Lithuania's first King, Mindaugas, was crowned in 1253, and was responsible for introducing Christianity to Lithuania and for establishing the Vilnius Cathedral. Most of the population, however, carried on worshipping the sun, tending fires, dancing in the woods, paying homage to bees and generally being pagan.

In 1323 Grand Duke Gediminas invited foreigners to settle in Vilnius with the promise of religious freedom, and later formed a union with Poland by marrying his daughter, Aldona, to the son of the then Polish king. These two moves, in what was one of the most influential periods in the history of Lithuania, resulted in the Lithuanian Polish kingdom flourishing and expanding. Teutonic knights attacked and were defeated in the battle of Žalgiris (also known as Tannenberg) in 1410.

In the 16th century the Lithuanian Polish dynasty weakened. Polish became the official state language, and wars with Russia and Sweden further weakened Lithuania. In 1795, Russia seized Vilnius and all but the western-most regions of Lithuania. The Russian occupation lasted 120 years, interrupted only by Napoleon and his army on their ill-fated campaign to Moscow in 1812.

The Russian occupation continued until the German occupation during World War I, but independence was declared in 1918. However, Vilnius was then attacked by Poland, which was under the impression that it belonged to them. Lithuania remained independent until Hitler and Stalin carved up Europe under the Molotov-Ribbentropp Pact. Almost all of the Lithuanian Jewish population was executed, and hordes of Lithuanians found themselves sent off to Siberia. Lithuanian partisans fled to the forest and waged guerrilla-style warfare against the Soviet occupation. They were hoping for a bit of help from the West, but never got it.

Lithuania declared independence again in 1990, but the Soviets did not listen, and in 1991 Soviet forces attempted to storm the Lithuanian parliament and TV tower. Fourteen people were killed. This time, however, the world took notice, and before long Soviet statues were being pulled down all over Lithuania.

This time Lithuania's bid for independence was realised. The country reintroduced its own currency, competed under its own flag at the Winter Olympics in 1992 and eventually joined the EU and NATO.

*There is a strong folk culture in Lithuania*

## Lifestyle

Despite having the highest suicide rate in the world, Lithuanians know how to have a good time – or at least the people who live in Vilnius do. Life here is tough for all but a wealthy few, and most people seem to spend a lot of time working, studying, or stressing about one or the other, or both. They do, however, squeeze in a cultural and social life. Theatres and concert halls are quite active, and the bars and restaurants that cater for locals are almost always buzzing.

Lithuanians know how to eat, drink and be merry and – contrary to the Russian cliché – enjoy their wonderful local beers as much as the shot of vodka.

Probably because Vilnius has a large student population, there are bars and nightclubs that are open all week, and they tend to stay open until around 02.00 or 03.00 early in the week, and until 05.00 on weekends. While there'll be plenty of places to have a drink, nightclubs don't seem to fire up until after 23.00. There are one or two places that, when the crowd is right and things are in full swing, simply don't bother closing. Certainly, Vilnius is a city that never sleeps, although things do slow down a bit in winter.

Living in Vilnius is cheap for western tourists and quite tough on a local wage – but that doesn't mean you can flounce around conducting yourself like some big-spending hotshot. There will be a few gormless hangers-on that will go for it, but mostly such behaviour will be met with resentment, cold shoulders and sneers.

Lithuanians tend to be a bit reserved and quiet, but are friendly, genuine and humble once you break the ice. They seem to welcome similar qualities in visitors.

A couple of final notes on cultural differences. Personal space and politeness are both more limited here than they are in the west (and especially Britain and Australia). If you're buying a bus or train ticket, or just waiting to get on a microbus, queue uncomfortably close to the person in front of you if you don't want someone else to push in, and don't be afraid to stand your ground. We certainly don't mean to suggest that more limited politeness is a good or bad thing – it's just different, and something you need to be aware of.

*Relaxing by the water's edge*

## Culture

Despite the fact that Vilnius is a small city, it has a lot to offer as far as culture goes. The theatre, opera and museums are often up to the standard of much bigger capitals. As a result of Vilnius's rich and complex history and location betwixt east and west, there is plenty to keep culture vultures satiated during a visit.

Arts were well funded during Soviet times, and the standard of education in the arts was very high. As a result, the standard of music, theatre and dance in Vilnius is good. Also, due to its location, Vilnius often attracts visiting artists from both east and west, providing a wealth of cultural experiences for visitors.

There isn't much to offer in terms of the non-performance arts, and while museums and galleries don't provide a good reason to come to Lithuania, they do provide a pleasant diversion if you're here anyway.

Before you even think of going to a museum, or to the opera or theatre, keep in mind that there are some fascinating cultural titbits scattered about in the streets. To some extent, Vilnius is a city of secrets. You could be right next to something of note, but not know it until you hear something of the story behind it. It's also possible to be in a drab and run-down looking corner of town, only to have a magnificent or quaint scene tucked away in a nearby courtyard or just around the corner. A guided tour, corny as it may sound, is worthwhile if you want to enhance your cultural experience of the city.

The Tourist Information Centre offers some good tours, and can even organise things like a traditional feast (where you get to slice

*Vilnius on a winter's day*

your dinner off a roast pig, use a lettuce leaf as a plate, and drink medieval mead from a clay tusk) or an evening of traditional dancing. It's all very authentic, but they can tend to go a bit over the top with theatrics. If you're a low profile, don't-look-at-me kind of person, walking around with a knight in shining armour or a very vocal monk with a fake beard might not be ideal.

There are also regular tours that you can just turn up to and join. Generally these start at the Cathedral at 10.00 and 15.00, but for current arrangements just check the ads in the regularly updated *Vilnius In Your Pocket* ⓦ www.inyourpocket.com

If you don't fancy the idea of following a group, you can get a private and alternative guide at a reasonable cost, and can then focus on particular areas of interest such as art, religion, graffiti, ghosts and legends or whatever takes your fancy. **Aventuras** is particularly good at putting together slightly offbeat and interesting tours.
ⓐ Literatų 8 ⓣ +370 5265 2355 ⓦ www.aventuras.lt

❶ One thing to keep in mind, however, is that the live performances culture scene almost completely shuts down over the summer period, which is when you might otherwise most like to visit. Museums stay open year-round, but can adopt some strange hours in summer.

*Higher Castle offers splendid views of the Old Town*

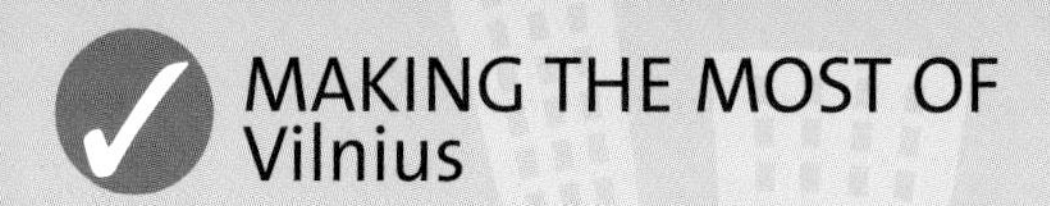

# MAKING THE MOST OF Vilnius

# Shopping

While many will say that Vilnius is a cheap city to visit, it's not a shopping destination. A shopping expedition, however, is still worthwhile from the experience point of view, especially if you head to some of the more old-fashioned markets.

On the top of Tauras Hill, in and around the Trade Union Palace, a market is held every Saturday morning that focuses on military memorabilia, collectables, and an assorted array of quirky junk. There are also old stamps, badges and coins inside – a must for keen collectors of any of those things.

The people who sell such stuff also make a regular appearance at the eastern edge of Kalvarijų Market – a more mainstream market that is held just out of town and where you can buy almost anything – goldfish, old boots, low-quality electronic paraphernalia with instructions in Russian, and fashion brand-name knock-offs that will come apart at the seams before you get home. There will even be little old ladies who will gladly sell you used plastic shopping bags from expensive fashion stores so, even if you've bought a complete load of rubbish, you can carry it with dignity.

Near the train station, there is a produce market where you can see people pushing around half a cow in a dented shopping trolley. It's actually a fascinating experience for the gourmand, and an eye-opener for anyone used to supermarkets.

While we're on the subject of supermarkets, there are two and a half options. Iki, Maxima and Rimi. Iki is a bit 'boutique' and sells a good range of otherwise hard-to-find goods. Maxima supermarkets are big and boring, except for the fact that their larger stores have fish tanks where you can buy live fish, such as carp. The other option is Rimi – fine if there's one nearby, but often there isn't.

There are three main modern shopping centres. Gedimino Prospektas is the main drag, so you'll go there anyway, but be aware that there are some nice shops tucked all the way down the western end. Europa is a new and modern shopping centre, but not very big and offers exactly what you would expect and nothing you don't. Akropolis is colossal by local standards, and is notable because it has an ice skating rink in the middle of it, so you can do your shopping, and then sit and eat pizza or sip coffee while you watch people falling over.

**USEFUL SHOPPING PHRASES**

**What time do the shops open/close?**
Kada atidaromos/uždaromos/parduotuvės?
*Kah-dah ah-teeh-dah-roh-mohs/uzh-darr-om-oss pahr-dot-oov-ess?*

**How much is this?**
Kiek šitas kainuoja?
*Keck sheetus kay-noh-ya?*

**Can I try this on?**
Ar galima pasimatuoti?
*Ur gull-im-uh pass-im-ah-totee?*

**My size is ...**
Mano numeris ...
*Mah-noh noo-mer-iss ...*

**I'll take this one, thank you**
Aš šitą paimsiu. Ačiū
Ash sheet-ah pah-im-soo. Ah-choo

**This is too large/too small/too expensive.**
**Do you have any others?**
Per didelis/per mažas/per brangus. Ar turite ką kitų?
*Perr did-el-iss/perr mazh-us/perr bran-goose. Ur toor-it-teh kah*

# Eating & drinking

Meat and potatoes, meat and potatoes, and more meat and potatoes. The local food is pretty basic, but generally of good quality (fresh and tasty) and good value. While locals have traditionally enjoyed a hot meal in the middle of the day, and office workers would often have lunch at a restaurant or café, the gradually increasing prices in restaurants are changing those habits.

A common meal would consist of a few pieces of battered and fried meat such as pork or chicken, some boiled potatoes, and a 'white salad' consisting of potatoes, peas and carrots in mayonnaise. Coleslaw can also often be found on the edge of the plate.

The Lithuanian national dish is *cepelinai*, or 'zeppelins'. While the dish probably originated from Germany, it is now a favourite in Lithuania. Cepelinai are football-shaped dumplings formed from a grated potato mixture wrapped around a small wad of spiced meat or curd. They are normally served with any of various sauces, and the different sauces represent different regional variations of the dish.

*Vederai* are another potato dish to put on the list of traditional foods to sample, although it must be said that they are more pleasing to eat than any description would suggest. Essentially, it's a length of a sheep's intestine filled with a creamy mashed potato, and grilled. Think of it as a potato sausage.

These traditional dishes are not just offerings for the tourists – they are still enjoyed by the locals, and are therefore available in a range of restaurants. They also tend to be good value, and probably offer more calories for your dollar than any fast-food outlet could.

International food is also widely available but tends to be more expensive, although, once again, the quality and value are excellent.

Lithuanians enjoy a drink, and will proudly remind you that the local brews often come away with medals and accolades from international beer competitions. The beer tends to be light, crisp, and easy to drink. Snacks are often enjoyed with beer, and it's a good idea to order some, since, while the beer may look light, its alcoholic

*Enjoy a drink while watching Vilnius life go by*

content is not. Popular beer snacks (*užkandžiai prie alaus*) include little sticks of fried dark bread (*kepinta duona*), onto which cheese is melted or garlic can be scraped. For the more adventurous, there are pigs' ears.

In both restaurants and bars, tipping is not required, but is a good reward for good service. Rounding up your bill to avoid small change or offering an extra ten percent or so is standard.

The whole restaurant scene takes on a different atmosphere in summer, when dozens of outdoor cafés and eateries appear, seemingly from nowhere, and fill streets and courtyards alike. Each of these venues is actually attached to a bricks-and-mortar venue, although it can be hard to tell which belongs to which – sometimes they're not even close together.

It can be very pleasant to sit outside at such venues until the late evening in summer – and as the days are very long, that can mean 22.00 or 23.00.

Possibly because of this outdoor café culture, picnics tend not to be popular in Vilnius, although Lithuanians do love to get out of town and visit one of the country's many lakes. Barbecues are common in the homes in villages around the lakes, although unless you're friendly with a local family, it would be hard to organise something like that unless you stay at a country cabin.

**RESTAURANT CATEGORIES**

Restaurants: Average price of a three-course meal (without drinks)

**£** = under 15Lt **££** = 15–25Lt

**£££** = over 25Lt

## USEFUL DINING PHRASES

**I would like a table for ... people**
Norėčiau staliuko ... žmonėms
*Norr-etch-ow stah-lyoo-koh ... zhmo-nems*

**May I have the bill, please?**
Ar galite atnešti sąskaitą?
*Ur gull-i-teh at-nesh-tee sass-kay-tah?*

**Waiter/waitress!**
Padavėjau! Padavėja!
*Pah-dah-veh-yau! Pah-dah-veh-yah!*

**Could I have it well-cooked/medium/rare, please?**
Ar galite iškepti visiškai/vidutiniškai/su krauju?
*Ur gull-it-eh ish-kept-ee wee-seesh-kay/wee-doo-teenie-shkay/soo crow-yoo?*

**I am a vegetarian. Does this contain meat?**
Aš vegetaras. Ar tai su mėsa?
*Ash veh-geh-tah-rahs. Ahr tay suh meh-sah?*

**Where is the toilet (restroom) please?**
Kur yra tualetas?
*Coor ee-ruh too-al-ett-us?*

**I would like a cup of/two cups of/another coffee/tea**
Prašom puodelį/du puodelius/dar kavos/arbatos
*Prash-om poh-deh-lee/doo poh-deh-loos/dahr kah-voss/ar-bat-oss*

# Entertainment & nightlife

## MUSIC, DRAMA & DANCE

One of the great joys of Vilnius is the quality and variety of performances that you can see without making a dent in your holiday budget. Lithuanians, despite having become a bit of a bad joke in the Eurovision Song Contest, do actually place a strong emphasis on music and theatre, and are proud to show off the excellent results.

In addition, touring artists often turn up in Vilnius, and you can sometimes catch some reasonably big-name international acts without the astronomical ticket prices that you might expect to pay at home. Older heavy metal and rock acts seem to have a habit of appearing here.

Theatre is varied and always of good quality, but it can be a bit baffling if it's in Lithuanian. Still, the creativity and energy with which it is performed still make it very interesting.
For information on upcoming performances, see Ⓦ www.eb.lt

Tickets can generally be purchased at the venue on the evening of the performance, or booked in advance on the internet. There is also a ticket booth in the public square opposite the Novotel Hotel on Gediminas Avenue.

In warmer months – May to August inclusive – you can also come across excellent music and dance in public spaces. Keep an eye on the Cathedral Square, the Town Hall Square, and the larger Old Town courtyards, especially on public holidays and festival days. Chances are you'll come across some traditional Lithuanian music and dance, which can be a real treat.

*A traditional instrument for a traditional town*

## Sport & relaxation

Basketball is not just a sport in Lithuania – it's pretty much a second religion. Visiting a game between rivals *Lietuvos Rytas* (the Vilnius team) and *Žalgiris* (from Kaunas) is the Lithuanian equivalent of seeing Real Madrid go against FC Barcelona in Spain. Lithuania's borders have been known to close when such a big game is on – it's quite an event. Even if you can't make it to a game, watching it live in any bar or club in Vilnius is also a great experience – especially if the Vilnius team wins. Football is also played, but is by no measure as popular as basketball. Schedules and tickets are available from the **Tiketa** website ⓦ www.tiketa.lt

For easy-going relaxation with friends, billiards and bowling are both common.

A local treat is the sauna and spa. Most good hotels in town have their own facilities that can be booked by the hour, usually at a special rate for guests. Another option is to head out of town to a sauna and spa in a village, which can be delightful, especially in winter when you can combine it with jumping about in the snow or plunging through a hole in a frozen lake. Not for everyone, admittedly, but certainly an adventure to tell your friends about. Local flavour can be added by getting yourself whacked and beaten by a leafy branch and having a honey massage. Be sure when you are booking a sauna that it is understood exactly what you want, and be aware that if you are quoted what seems like an exorbitantly high price, you are probably being offered 'company', not just the use of the sauna.

Because Lithuania is a land of many lakes and rivers, canoeing and kayaking are a great way to explore and pass time. You can even combine this with camping for a pleasant and quite unique holiday.

There are companies that specialise in sorting out such adventures:
**Aventuras** ⓐ Literatų 8 ⓣ +370 5265 2355 ⓦ www.aventuras.lt
**Active Holidays** ⓣ +370 6872 1847 ⓦ www.activeholidays.lt

*Basketball is enjoyed by Lithuanians of all ages*

## Accommodation

There is a good range of hotels in Vilnius, covering everything with the exception of the silly high end of the market. There are certainly hotels that lay the luxury on in abundance and offer a good-value treat, but there are also more cosy affairs that have plenty of charm without the high prices. Self-catering apartments and B&B-style accommodation are also available, and offer excellent value for

*The Romeo and Juliet room at the Shakespeare Boutique Hotel*

those who don't mind – or prefer – being a bit more independent. Budget travellers can choose from a small selection of hostels that are pretty basic, but are earning a reputation for offering a fun and friendly atmosphere.

All the best hotels accept bookings online, while some of the smaller places, including apartments and B&Bs, lack online commerce facilities but will accept email enquiries and require you to fill out a form and fax it back in order to actually make the booking.

You can just turn up unannounced at hostels and get a bed in all but the summer season (June to August inclusive), but be aware that Vilnius is growing in popularity very quickly, especially with adventure-seeking budget travellers, and this situation could have changed by the time you read this. It's best to book.

## HOSTELS

**AA Hostel £** The newest hostel, but a bit cramped and somehow feeling a bit un-lived-in and short-term – although we're sure that will change as more people discover it and leave dents in the bedposts and socks behind the cupboards. The location is arguably the best of all the hostels, halfway between the train and bus station area and the centre of Old Town. ⓐ Šv. Stepono 15 ⓣ +370 6801 8557 ⓦ www.ahostel.lt

**PRICE RATING**

Hotels: Average price of a room for two

**£** = under 150Lt **££** = 150ff–400Lt

**£££** = over 400Lt

**Filaretai £** The furthest away from all the action, but located in the funky and alternative Užupis district. Walking to or from this hostel is half the fun, except if you're alone and it's very late at night. This one is a part of the IYH network, and also has bicycles available for hire. ⓐ Filaretų 17 ⓣ +370 5215 4627 ⓦ www.filaretaihostel.lt

**Old Town Hostel £** Small, comfortable, friendly, well located and well run. There used to be all sorts of stories on backpacker internet forums about the antics that the owner of this place would get up to, but most of them were far-fetched and he's gone anyway. Still, the place is worth staying at, even without the fanciful stories. ⓐ Aušros Vartų 20–10 ⓣ +370 5262 5357

**APARTMENTS & B&B**

**Litinterp £–££** Long-serving in Vilnius, and the experts on getting you in basic but comfortable digs without denting your budget. They can also offer home-stay accommodation, and a range of other services for travellers. Their reputation for dealing with all manner of requests is second to none, and their status as being the best for those on a budget is well deserved. ⓐ Bernardinų 7-2 ⓣ +370 5212 3850 ⓦ www.litinterp.lt

**HOTELS**

**Shakespeare Boutique Hotel ££** Vilnius's best boutique-style hotel, tucked away in a quiet backstreet, but within view of all the main attractions. Rooms are named after, and themed upon, famous authors and literary characters. Guess what the Romeo & Juliet room is good for? It's the sort of place where regular visitors tend to settle on their favourite room and request it each time they come, and it is also certainly the case that the decorations and friendliness of the staff offer a home-away-from-home quality to the place. ⓐ Bernardinų 8/8 ⓣ +370 5266 5885 ⓦ www.shakespeare.lt

**CityPark £££** Right on the corner of the Cathedral Square, and a good compromise between being a boring business-style box and a very homely place to stay. Every room is a bit different and has unique facilities. Some have separate bath and shower, some have just a shower, some have split-beds (a double made from two singles pushed together) while others have big single-mattress beds. Just be sure to be specific about what you want and it's unlikely that you will be disappointed. Don't miss the spa and sauna facilities hidden away downstairs. ⓐ Stuokos-Gucevičiaus 3 ⓣ +370 5212 3515 ⓦ www.citypark.lt

**Europa Royale Vilnius £££** The Italian interior designers obviously had fun, and so will you in this ostentatious and opulent hideaway. It may appear to be a bit over the top to those of subtle and refined tastes, but the nouveau riche will love it. If you're not so keen on glitz and don't want to find gold sequins under your bed, opt for the standard rooms with their more subdued decoration. In any case, the level of appointments and service is excellent. ⓐ Aušros Vartų 6 ⓣ +370 5266 0770 ⓦ www.groupeuropa.com

**Narutis £££** You're really getting something special here, and not just due to the outstanding location. The rooms have all been decorated by a French interior designer, all have their own particular character, all have frescoes, and all have elements of the Olde Worlde (well, 16th century, anyway) building exposed to add character. On top of that there are all the usual offerings of a fine hotel. ⓐ Pilies 24 ⓣ +370 5212 2894 ⓦ www.narutis.com

**Novotel £££** In what is known as one of the ugliest buildings in Old Town are some of the niftiest rooms – some with great views. All the rooms here follow a standard design used in the newer Novotel hotels worldwide, so you may know exactly what to expect. It's minimalist, a bit Scandinavian-looking, and with everything you could need tucked neatly away somewhere. Note that this hotel has a room specifically fitted out for disabled visitors, which overlooks the interior of a shopping centre. It's often vacant, and therefore a good target for last-minute haggling. ⓐ Gedimino 16 ⓣ +370 5266 6200 ⓦ www.novotel.com

**Radisson SAS Astorija £££** The US President, George W Bush, stayed here – make of that what you will. The building is charming, and the rooms all have a somewhat strict and squared-off style that offers an air of efficiency and formality. Don't let that put you off, however, as there are plenty of armchairs with plump cushions and no shortage of that crisp-linen comfort that one finds in a big fresh bed. The location is also very good, being right at the intersection of two of the main tourist streets, and tucked away behind the town hall. ⓐ Didžioji 35/2 ⓣ +370 5212 0110 ⓦ www.vilnius.radissonsas.com

**Stikliai £££** Exquisite in every respect, with a very refined but charming French feel. Or is it Spanish? Anyway, this is the place to take someone if you really want to impress, and it is so good that it is often booked out by diplomats, high-flyers, and others with expensive tastes and budgets to match. Small-time criminals with floozy hangers-on don't get much of a look-in here. ⓐ Gaono 7 ⓣ +370 5264 9595 ⓦ www.stikliaihotel.lt

*The famous Three Crosses*

# THE BEST OF VILNIUS

Getting the most out of Vilnius requires an open mind, a desire to explore, a pair of feet and the willingness to use them. Often the best things are somewhat hidden in a tucked-away courtyard or behind a door that may not look too inviting. There tend not to be flashing neon signs beckoning you to come hither, or even signs that say 'welcome' on the doors of good restaurants. Do be inquisitive, and don't be shy.

**TOP 10 ATTRACTIONS**

- **St Anne's Church** The prettiest thing in Vilnius – architecturally speaking, anyway – even if the inside is a bit dull (see page 64).

- **Cathedral** Just browse, or book an in-depth tour of the cellars (see page 62).

- **KGB Museum (Genocide Victims' Museum)** Stoic, grim and even a bit sickening – but essential (see page 64).

- **Gedimino Pilis – (Higher Castle Museum)** Even if only for the view from the top (see page 68).

- **Applied Art Museum** All Vilnius' treasures are tucked away in here, along with some very serious security guards (see pages 66–7).

- **A wander around Old Town** Charming streets, quirky courtyards, inviting cafés, and a myriad ways to get lost (see pages 62–79).

- **Traditional meal in a cellar** Burrow into Lokys (Stiklių 8) or Žemaičiai (Vokiečių 24) for *cepelinai* in a cellar (see page 74).

- **A market** They'll try to sell you anything. A trip to a market can be like a jaunt in a time machine – and it's free (see page 95).

- **Užupis** The so-called funky and alternative area, and breakaway independent republic (see page 80). Look for the constitution on the wall (Paupio Gatvė – angel end).

- **Gates of Dawn** Try not to trip over the little old ladies who kneel in the street to pray.

The Cathedral dominates the Old Town

Your at-a-glance guide to seeing the best that Vilnius has to offer, depending on how much time you have.

**HALF-DAY: VILNIUS IN A HURRY**

When you're pushed for time, concentrate on the area around the Cathedral. Here you can visit the castle on top of the hill, the National Museum, the Museum of Applied Art, and of course the Cathedral itself. Finish off by wandering up and down Pilies Street – to the Town Hall and back – and stop off for a quick lunch or coffee at any of the many cafés.

**1-DAY: TIME TO SEE A LITTLE MORE**

With a little more time, you can explore Old Town more – and that means just walking. You can head in pretty much any direction from the Town Hall and find yourself in a network of charming streets. The mixture of charming and decrepit delights you will come across is delightful. If you have an interest in Jewish history and culture, head south towards Geto Square and keep your eyes peeled for plaques with Yiddish inscriptions along the way.

*You're likely to witness some traditional dancing while in Vilnius*

## 2–3 DAYS: SHORT CITY BREAK

Squeezing in a trip to Trakai is a must – it's home to a medieval-looking castle nestled on an island in a lake, with pretty greenery on all the surrounding banks. It's the sort of scene that postcards were made for. Buses to Trakai leave the Vilnius bus station every half-hour or so, and the journey takes about half an hour. When you get off the bus in Trakai, you have to walk for about twenty minutes in the same direction the bus was heading, follow a bend in the road, and then you will come across the main part of the settlement and the iconic castle. You can also catch a taxi from Vilnius to Trakai for something in the order of 50 litas, but getting a cab to take you back can be a nuisance as taxi drivers are reluctant to drive out there just to pick up a one-way fare.

## LONGER: ENJOYING VILNIUS TO THE FULL

In summer, it would be a shame to spend any time in Lithuania without exploring nature, and in particular the national parks and lakes. A trip to the unique UNESCO World Heritage-listed Curonian Spit is also a must, and you might like to pop the Hill of Crosses in Šiauliai on the list too, although both are some distance out of Vilnius and would require an overnight stay. Closer to Vilnius are Kernavė and Molėtai, the former of which boasts some interesting history, and the latter of which is known as an area of many gorgeous lakes.

Finally, if you have a day to spare, consider jumping on a bus and heading to Gruto Parkas, near to Druskininkai. This is a theme park where many of Lithuania's old Soviet statues of Lenin and Stalin have found their home. More details are available in the section on Druskininkai.

# Something for nothing

The best way to enjoy Vilnius without spending a cent – or a *centas*, as the locals would say – is to walk. Exploring Old Town is a very rewarding experience, especially if you deviate from the obvious routes and burrow into little side streets and courtyards. Slip through what may look like a private doorway, and you can discover a whole new side of the city, where one courtyard adjoins another, and then another, before leading to another street.

On Vokiečių Street next door to the Žemaičiai restaurant, for example, is a little doorway that leads to a courtyard that, with parked cars and the back doors of restaurants, is hardly much of a discovery. At the back of this courtyard, however, is a little tunnel – you'll have to crouch to get through it – that leads to another courtyard that is well worth discovering. It's a pleasant snapshot of a different way of life. Wooden balconies overlook the yard where sometimes locals sit and chat. A line of wooden storage sheds lines another side of the courtyard. You've probably only walked 50 metres, but you'll feel a million miles away from the hustle and bustle of Vokiečių Street.

Another courtyard, on Rūdninkių Street near the corner of Pylimo, boasts an almost intact portion of the otherwise long-gone original city wall.

The routes through these courtyards are not marked on any map, as essentially they are private property. Keep this in mind as you explore. Essentially you are walking through someone's back yard, so keep quiet, and don't hang around in one spot gawking into windows for too long. Act with respect for the locals and you won't have a problem, and nor will they.

Vilnius also puts on a great show for the skint every now and then, with free concerts and celebrations in the Cathedral Square.

If you're in town on any of the public holidays, you'll probably be able to join a crowd for a free and fun evening from about 19.00.

Also explore public spaces, especially Cathedral Square, Gedimino Prospektas and Rutožės (Town Hall) Square, on national days as there are often markets and fairs where you can try traditional foods, and see various costumes and dancing.

If you're in Vilnius on April Fools' Day, you'd be a fool not to head to Užupis, the self-declared independent republic breakaway district. They'll be happy to stamp your passport and toss you into the midst of all sorts of wacky revelry on that day. Or maybe not. Depends what kind of mood they're in.

*What a contrast! Notice the TV tower in the background*

## When it rains

There's a whole other side of Vilnius to explore when the skies open up – the underside. Vilnius is riddled with cellars and crypts. Most have been turned into cafés, bars, nightclubs and so on, that play on the cave-like appeal of their location. Others are museums, and others are – well – just plain creepy. Burrowing into such places is an excellent option in bad weather.

The most obvious underground attraction is the network of crypts and rooms beneath the main Cathedral. Reasonably priced tours can be organised at the small shop located in the side of the Cathedral. Group tours are best value, so if you have or can find some travelling companions you should plan to go together. Otherwise tours leave at specified times, and you'll join others then. Times, prices and information are available from the staff at the shop who may or may not speak English, depending on when you go. If you have trouble, just drop into one of the Tourist Information Centres and ask them to make arrangements by phone for you.

We won't give away too much, but a tour beneath the Cathedral covers architectural, artistic and political history in a very practical kind of way (see pages 62–4).

Another underground attraction is the Artillery Bastion – a horseshoe-shaped tunnel in the side of a hill. While it's pretty obvious that this was built for defensive purposes (it was once a part of the original city wall), it's also worth noting, as you explore, that it has also been used to store vegetables, garbage and orphaned children. Entrance costs less than a cup of coffee, probably because there's not too much to see or do down there, but it is worth a visit all the same.

More varied and rewarding is the National Museum. Of course, it's not underground, but it has plenty of bits and pieces that once were. Old coins, bits of Napoleon's troops' uniforms, and a wide variety of other artefacts have been relieved from the earth and presented here, along with informative descriptions in English.

*The airport building is mostly in keeping with the architectural style*

# On arrival

Lithuania is a member of the European Union and, at the time of writing, working towards membership of the Schengen Agreement. It's in a time zone two hours ahead of Greenwich Mean Time, and the clocks go forward one hour for daylight saving in March, and back again in October.

When it's midday in summer in Vilnius, the time elsewhere is as follows:

**Australia** Eastern Standard Time 19.00, Central Standard Time 18.30, Western Standard Time 17.00

**New Zealand** 21.00

**South Africa** 11.00

**UK and Republic of Ireland** 10.00

**USA and Canada** Newfoundland Time 06.30, Atlantic Canada Time 06.00, Eastern Time 05.00, Central Time 04.00, Mountain Time 03.00, Pacific Time 02.00, Alaska 01.00.

**By air**

**Vilnius Airport**

Vilnius Airport is a small and uncomplicated facility, just a 15-minute taxi ride from the centre of Old Town. Immigration and customs won't hold you up much (unless you're doing something or carrying something that would warrant more than the usual attention) and you'll soon find yourself in a square hall full of family and friends (but not yours), holding flowers. The ATM is on the wall to your right, and if you're arriving during business hours you can find a kiosk by exploring the hallway in the same direction. The kiosk can help you out with things like periodical guide books (we recommend *Vilnius In Your Pocket* for its up-to-date listings of venues and cultural

events), phone cards for public phones, pre-paid SIM cards for your mobile phone, public transport tickets, cigarettes, chewing gum, newspapers that you won't understand, and so on.

Taxi drivers from the Martonas company have been granted a licence to hassle you as you emerge from the arrivals hall. They will try to charge you something in the order of 25–50Lt to take you to Old Town. Even considering the possible inflation during the life of this guide, you shouldn't pay more.

To the left as you emerge from the airport is a bus stop, where buses 1 and 2 will take you to town for a mere 1.40Lt. You can buy a ticket from the driver, who probably won't speak English.

**Kaunas Airport**

If you're arriving at Kaunas airport with the intention of travelling on to Vilnius, you'll have to go to Kaunas itself and then take a bus

*An easy way to get around*

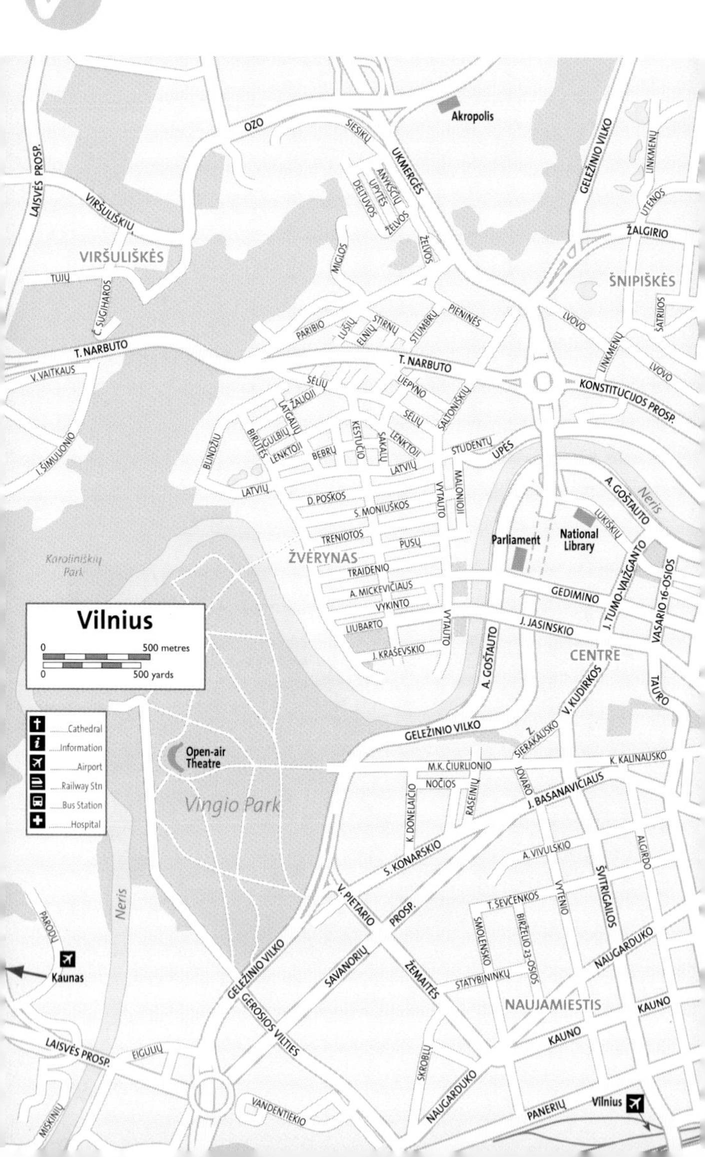

Vilnius
0 500 metres
0 500 yards
Cathedral
Information
Airport
Railway Stn
Bus Station
Hospital
Akropolis
VIRŠULIŠKĖS
ŠNIPIŠKĖS
ŽVĖRYNAS
CENTRE
NAUJAMIESTIS
Karoliniškių Park
Vingio Park
Open-air Theatre
Parliament
National Library
Neris
Kaunas
Vilnius
OZO
ŠIESIKŲ
UKMERGĖS
LAISVĖS PROSP.
VIRŠULIŠKIŲ
TUJŲ
Č. SUGIHAROS
T. NARBUTO
V. VAITKAUS
I. ŠIMULIONIO
GELEŽINIO VILKO
LINKMENŲ
UTENOS
ŽALGIRIO
LVOVO
ŠATRIJOS
KONSTITUCIJOS PROSP.
PIENINĖS
STUMBRŲ
STIRNŲ
ELNIŲ
LUŠIŲ
PARIBIO
MIGLOS
ŽELVOS
DELTUVOS
UPYTĖS
ANYKŠČIŲ
ŠELIŲ
ŽALIOJI
LATGALIŲ
LIEPYNO
SALTONIŠKIŲ
BLINDŽIŲ
BIRUTĖS
GULBIŲ
LENKTOJI
BEBRŲ
KESTUČIO
SAKALŲ
LATVIŲ
STUDENTŲ
UPĖS
A. GOŠTAUTO
LUKIŠKIŲ
D. POŠKOS
S. MONIUŠKOS
VYTAUTO
MALONIOJI
TRENIOTOS
PUŠŲ
TRAIDENIO
A. MICKEVIČIAUS
VYKINTO
LIUBARTO
J. KRAŠEVSKIO
GEDIMINO
J. JASINSKIO
J. TUMO-VAIŽGANTO
VASARIO 16-OSIOS
TAURO
V. KUDIRKOS
Z. SIERAKAUSKO
M.K. ČIURLIONIO
K. KALINAUSKO
NOČIOS
RASEINIŲ
K. DONELAIČIO
JOVARO
J. BASANAVIČIAUS
A. VIVULSKIO
ALGIRDO
S. KONARSKIO
V. PIETARIO
PROSP.
T. ŠEVČENKOS
VYTENIO
ŠVITRIGAILOS
SMOLENSKO
BIRŽELIO 23-OSIOS
NAUGARDUKO
STATYBININKŲ
SAVANORIŲ
ŽEMAITĖS
KAUNO
GEROSIOS VILTIES
PARODŲ
LAISVĖS PROSP.
EIGULIŲ
SKROBLŲ
MIŠKINIŲ
VANDENTIEKIO
PANERIŲ

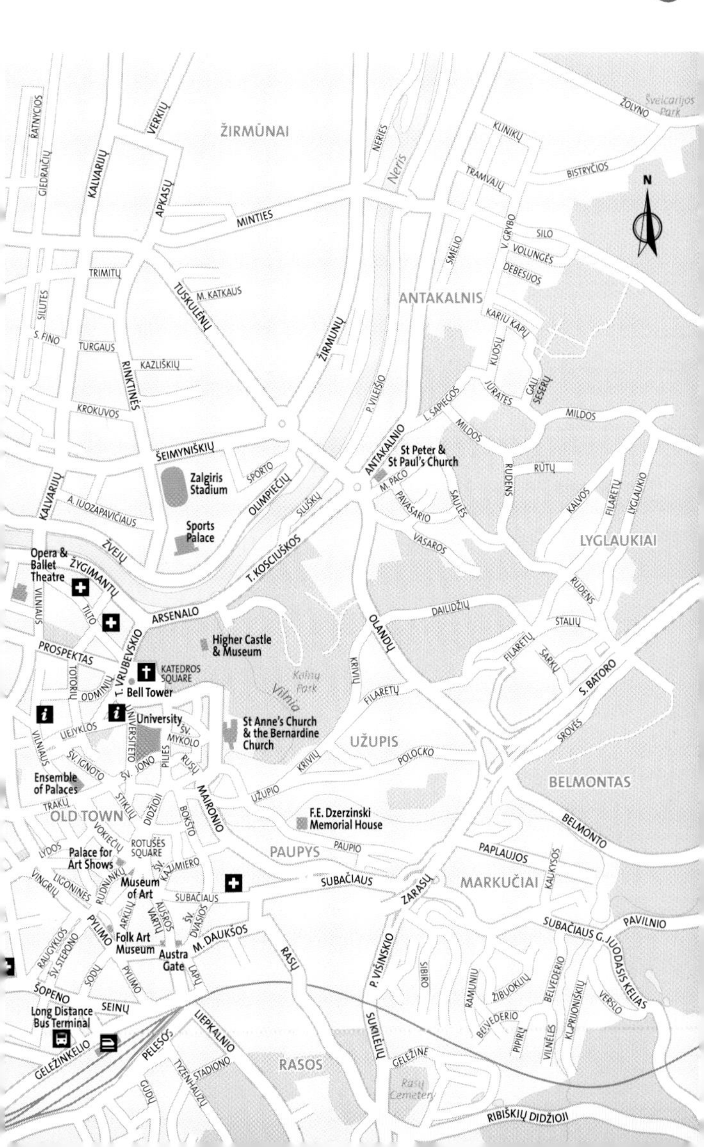
ŽIRMŪNAI
ANTAKALNIS
LYGLAUKIAI
UŽUPIS
BELMONTAS
PAUPYS
MARKUČIAI
OLD TOWN
RASOS
N
Neris
Vilnia
Kalnų Park
Šveicarijos Park
Rasų Cemetery
Opera & Ballet Theatre
Zalgiris Stadium
Sports Palace
St Peter & St Paul's Church
Higher Castle & Museum
KATEDROS SQUARE
Bell Tower
University
St Anne's Church & the Bernardine Church
Ensemble of Palaces
F.E. Dzerzinski Memorial House
Palace for Art Shows
ROTUŠĖS SQUARE
Museum of Art
Folk Art Museum
Austra Gate
Long Distance Bus Terminal
RATNYČIOS
GIEDRAIČIŲ
KALVARIJŲ
VERKIŲ
APKASŲ
MINTIES
NERIES
KLINIKŲ
TRAMVAJŲ
BISTRYČIOS
ŽOLYNO
SILO
VOLUNGĖS
DEBESIJOS
V. GRYBO
SMĖLIO
TRIMITŲ
TUSKULĖNŲ
M. KATKAUS
ŠILUTĖS
S. FINO
TURGAUS
KAZLIŠKIŲ
RINKTINĖS
KROKUVOS
ŽIRMŪNŲ
P. VILEIŠIO
KARIŲ KAPŲ
KUOSŲ
JŪRATĖS
L. SAPIEGOS
MILDOS
ŠEIMYNIŠKIŲ
SPORTO
OLIMPIEČIŲ
ANTAKALNIO
M. PACO
PAVASARIO
SAULĖS
RUDENS
RŪTŲ
KALVOS
FILARETŲ
LYGLAUKIO
A. IUOZAPAVIČIAUS
ŽVEJŲ
SLUŠKŲ
T. KOSCIUŠKOS
VASAROS
ŽYGIMANTŲ
VILNIAUS
TILTO
ARSENALO
DAILIDŽIŲ
STALIŲ
OLANDŲ
PROSPEKTAS
T. VRUBLEVSKIO
TOTORIŲ
ODMINIŲ
KRIVIŲ
ŠARKŲ
S. BATORO
SROVĖS
LIEJYKLOS
UNIVERSITETO
ŠV. MYKOLO
ŠV. IGNOTO
ŠV. JONO
PILIES
RUSŲ
POLOCKO
UŽUPIO
TRAKŲ
STIKLIŲ
DIDŽIOJI
BOKŠTO
MAIRONIO
BELMONTO
VOKIEČIŲ
LYDOS
PAUPIO
PAPLAUJOS
KAUKYSOS
ŠV. KAZIMIERO
VINGRIŲ
LIGONINĖS
RŪDNINKŲ
SUBAČIAUS
ZARASŲ
ARKLIŲ
AUŠROS VARTŲ
ŠV. DVASIOS
PYLIMO
M. DAUKŠOS
SUBAČIAUS G.
PAVILNIO
JUODASIS KELIAS
RAUGYKLOS
ŠV. STEPONO
SODŲ
RASŲ
P. VIŠINSKIO
SIBIRO
RAMUNIŲ
ŽIBUOKLIŲ
BELVEDERIO
KLPRIJONIŠKIŲ
VERSLO
ŠOPENO
SEINŲ
LAPŲ
LIEPKALNIO
SUKILĖLIŲ
PIPIRŲ
VILNELĖS
GELEŽINKELIO
PELESOS
TYZENHAUZŲ
STADIONO
GUDŲ
GELEŽINĖ
RIBIŠKIŲ DIDŽIOJI

or train from there. Bus 29 goes from the airport to Kaunas bus and train stations, from where you can carry on to Vilnius. If your flight arrives late in the evening (after about 20.00), you'll miss the last buses and trains for Vilnius, so you'll have to arrange to stay the night in Kaunas, or pay about 200Lt for a taxi to Vilnius.

You may also like to stop for a while in Kaunas – Lithuania's second largest city – before you head on to Vilnius. For accommodation, maps and public transport information, as well as a list of things to do in Kaunas, pick up a copy of *Kaunas In Your Pocket*.

**By bus**

The bus station is not in the most pleasant part of town, so you probably won't want to hang around too long. When you get off a bus, walk through the bus station building itself and you'll find yourself on a big concrete apron. Walk straight ahead, veering to the right, and you'll find the train station over the road to your right, and a McDonald's over the road straight ahead. To walk to town, walk past McDonald's and carry on down the gentle slope until you come to a T-intersection with a rail bridge to the right. Turn left here and walk straight ahead. You'll soon pass through the Gates of Dawn into Old Town.

The bus station has facilities for left luggage, offices for international bus companies, kiosks, cafés and so on, but no currency exchange. If you need to get some local cash, we suggest using an ATM, otherwise you'll need to go to the train station for bureaux de change.

**By train**

Turning up on a train is trouble-free, unless you're arriving on an international train, in which case you will have to pass through customs. ATMs are located in the upper level of the train station, and there is a kiosk downstairs. When you walk out of the train station, you'll see a McDonald's opposite – see the details for arriving by bus, above, for directions on how to get to town from there.

## FINDING YOUR FEET

Vilnius is a relatively small and calm city, although there is also always plenty going on – especially in summer. It's the ideal city for strolling, but you need to be careful on narrow streets where pedestrians often spill onto the road, and the road seems to be used as a racetrack by cars, taxis and motorbikes. Smaller moped-style motorbikes are allowed on the footpaths, and tend to be ridden by

### IF YOU GET LOST, TRY ...

**Excuse me, do you speak English?**
Atsiprašau, Jūs kalbate angliškai?
*Aht-see-prah-show, Yoos kahl-bah-teh ahng-leesh-kay?*

**Excuse me, is this the right way to ... the cathedral/the tourist office/the castle/the old town?**
Atsiprašau, ar aš teisingai einu į ... katedrą/turistų biurą/pilį/senamiestį?
*Aht-see-prah-show, ur ash tey-sing-ay ay-noo ee ... cutt-ed-rah/too-riss-too byoo-rah/peeli/seh-nah-myes-tee?*

**Can you point to it on my map?**
Ar galite parodyti žemėlapyje?
*Ur gull-it-teh purr-oddity zhe-mell-uppie-ya?*

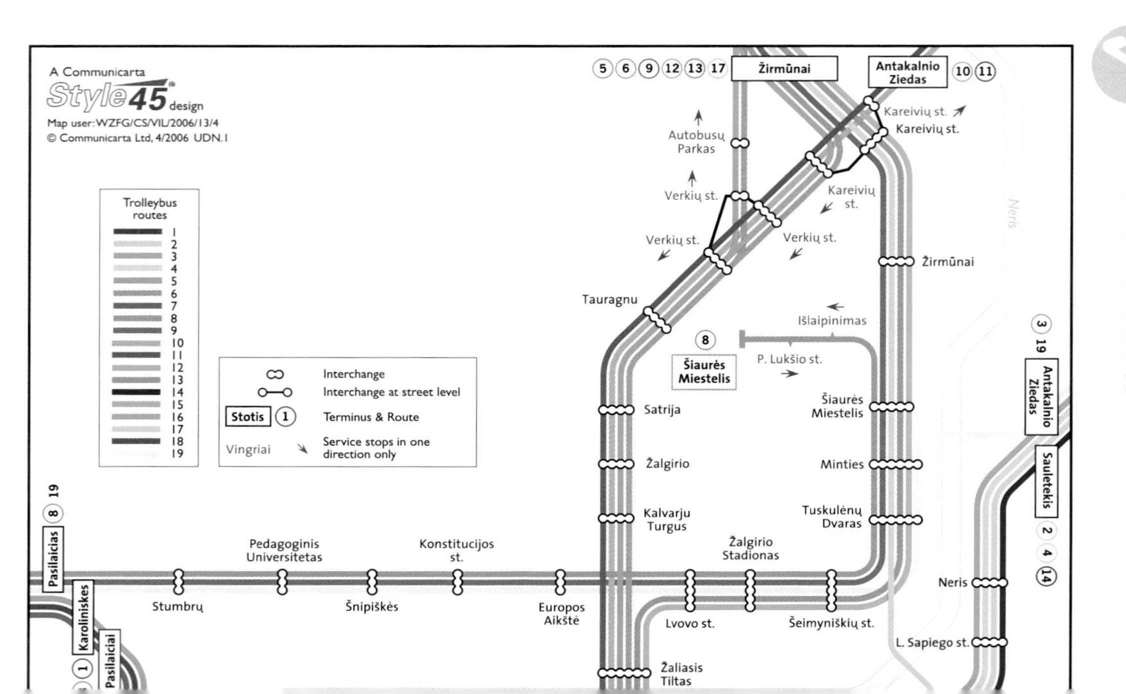
A Communicarta
Style45 design
Map user: WZFG/CS/VIL/2006/13/4
© Communicarta Ltd, 4/2006 UDN.1
Trolleybus routes
1
2
3
4
5
6
7
8
9
10
11
12
13
14
15
16
17
18
19
Interchange
Interchange at street level
Stotis 1 Terminus & Route
Vingriai Service stops in one direction only
5 6 9 12 13 17 Žirmūnai
Antakalnio Ziedas 10 11
Kareivių st.
Kareivių st.
Autobusų Parkas
Verkių st.
Kareivių st.
Verkių st.
Verkių st.
Žirmūnai
Neris
Tauragnu
Išlaipinimas
8 Šiaurės Miestelis
P. Lukšio st.
3 19 Antakalnio Ziedas
Satrija
Šiaurės Miestelis
Žalgirio
Minties
Sauletekis 2 4 14
Kalvarju Turgus
Tuskulėnų Dvaras
Pasilaicias 8 19
Pedagoginis Universitetas
Konstitucijos st.
Žalgirio Stadionas
Neris
Stumbrų
Šnipiškės
Europos Aikštė
Lvovo st.
Šeimyniškių st.
Karoliniskes 1
Pasilaiciai
L. Sapiego st.
Žaliasis Tiltas

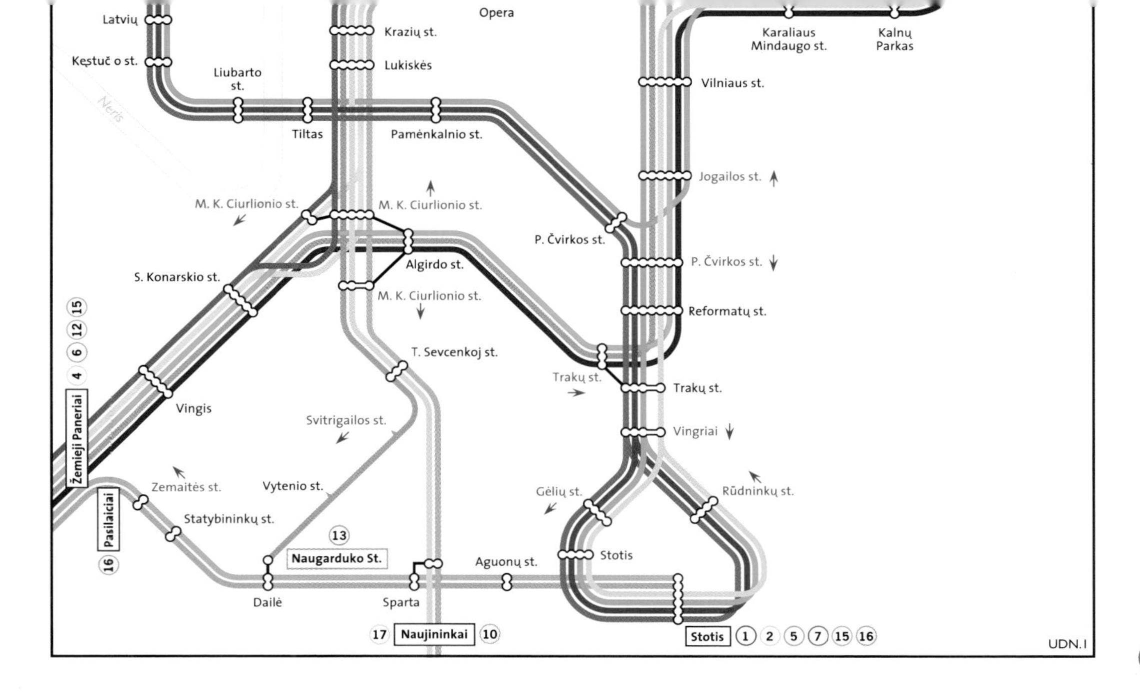

Latvių
Kęstuč o st.
Liubarto st.
Tiltas
Kražių st.
Lukiskės
Pamėnkalnio st.
Opera
Karaliaus Mindaugo st.
Kalnų Parkas
Vilniaus st.
Jogailos st.
M. K. Ciurlionio st.
M. K. Ciurlionio st.
P. Čvirkos st.
P. Čvirkos st.
Algirdo st.
S. Konarskio st.
M. K. Ciurlionio st.
Reformatų st.
T. Sevcenkoj st.
Trakų st.
Trakų st.
Vingis
Svitrigailos st.
Vingriai
Zemaitės st.
Vytenio st.
Gėlių st.
Rūdninkų st.
Statybininkų st.
13
Stotis
Naugarduko St.
Aguonų st.
Dailė
Sparta
Žemieji Paneriai
4 6 12 15
Pasilaiciai
16
17
Naujininkai
10
Stotis
1 2 5 7 15 16
UDN.I

teenagers with something to prove to the world and with no regard for pedestrians at all. Thankfully, they're noisy so you can hear them coming.

Crime against tourists is almost unheard of, but you do need to exercise common sense – keep valuables on your person, don't advertise whatever wealth you may have, and don't be rude to locals. Wearing a loud Hawaiian shirt or football top, dangling expensive technology around your neck, and saying 'Wow' and 'Hey' a lot in a loud voice is asking for trouble – especially at night.

Beggars are a problem. They are persistent in a way that many tourists are simply not used to. The Tourist Information Office has advised tourists not to offer money. In the summer of 2005, it produced small cards that were being offered to tourists to give to beggars. The cards detailed information about homeless shelters, soup kitchens and charitable organisations. Handing out a card was thought one way to make them go away. If this scheme is not continued, the best way to deal with beggars is with a firm 'NO!' – after which you should simply ignore them.

**ORIENTATION**

Vilnius sprawls out from around the Cathedral – a place where two rivers once met in a gentle valley. The smaller river *Vilnia* actually once flowed along the path of the road that you can now see in front of the Cathedral (Šventaragio).

Now, most of the bits of Vilnius that you'll be interested in fall into an area the shape of a generous pie-wedge, with the Cathedral being at the point. One edge is formed by the not quite straight line formed by Pilies, Didžioji and Aušros Vartų streets – although the area immediately to the east of that line should be included. The other edge is simply the long, straight Gedimino Prospektas. As we said, it's a very generous slice of pie – about two-thirds of a pie, to be precise.

The area of the Cathedral is a good orientation point, and a good place to head for if you get lost – everyone can point you in the right direction if you just say the word 'Cathedral'.

The streets of Vilnius, with the exception of the long and straight Gedimino Prospektas, are confusingly higgledy-piggledy. They were laid out in medieval days with the aid of a bent stick and a few generous tusks of mead. If your sense of direction is even slightly less than high-grade military GPS standard, don't go too far without a map until you get to know at least the main streets.

## GETTING AROUND

For the few instances when something is too far away to stroll to, Vilnius's comprehensive public transport system will get you there quickly and cheaply, except during the rush hour when you just get queue-jumped and may have to stand for a while pressed closely to either a bevy of catwalk angels or a lumpy and smelly pensioner with a sack full of onions. Pot luck, really.

There are trolleybuses, buses and microbuses. The trolleybuses are the ones with antennae that attach to cables above the road and make electric whirring noises as they creep along. Their routes tend to be mainly central, and are marked in red on the transport map. Regular buses – the ones that run on diesel – tend to travel a little further into the outskirts. Their routes are marked in blue. Be aware that a trolleybus and regular bus can have the same number, but go to completely different destinations. Make sure you get on the right one.

Tickets for trolleybuses and buses are the same, and can be purchased from kiosks marked *Lietuvos Spauda* or from the driver. You pay more when you buy from the driver. Each ticket is valid for a single journey on a single vehicle, and must be validated in either the electronic or the older red 'crimping' devices on board.

Microbuses are licensed, commercially run, and terribly convenient. They are just minibuses – transit vans full of seats – that tear along the numbered routes, picking up and dropping off passengers as required along the way. When you see one coming, you can hail it like you see people hailing a New York cab in movies – although you don't yell 'Taxi!' of course, because it's not a taxi. When you get in, pay the driver two litas (a price that we expect will increase during the life of this guidebook). When you approach your destination, simply make it known that you want to get off. If the driver doesn't understand 'I would like to get out here', just yell 'chair' a lot (it means 'here' in Lithuanian) and head for the door; the message will get across.

Taxis are cheap but, strangely, you'll pay less if you call to book a taxi than if you hail one in the street. A trip within the Old Town shouldn't cost more than 15 litas (about €5). A couple of reputable companies are Martonas (t 240 00 04) and Vilniaus Taksi (t 212 88 88).

Buses to other cities and locations in Lithuania and abroad leave regularly from the bus station. Trains tend to be less frequent, sometimes slower, sometimes full of shady characters drinking stinky substances out of plastic bottles, and about the same price as a bus. In summer, tickets for longer-distance bus travel should be purchased in advance from the Eurolines office in the bus station.

*The Cathedral's belltower is a striking landmark*

Otherwise you can just turn up and try your luck buying tickets from the driver.

## CAR HIRE

While Lithuania has a great network of buses provided by private companies, and they can get you pretty much anywhere, hiring a car is a great way to explore with a little less hassle and a lot more freedom. Navigating Lithuania is a breeze, with excellent road signs making it almost impossible to get lost.

In and around cities, however, driving can be a bit stressful as Lithuanian drivers are simply crazy – they appear to ignore road markings and overtake where there is no room to do so. Once you're on the open road, however, this is probably going to be more of a problem for them than it is for you. Keep an eye out for the odd bit of random traffic of the horse-and-cart or antiquated agricultural machinery type.

Most international car rental companies operate in Lithuania, with a couple of cheaper local options as well.

**Avis** ⓐ Laisvės 3 ⓣ +370 5232 9316 ⓦ www.avis.lt
**Budget** ⓐ Rodūnios Kelias 2 (Airport) ⓣ +370 5230 6708 (24hrs) ⓦ www.budget.lt
**Europcar** ⓐ Stuokos-Gucevičiaus 9-1 ⓣ +370 5212 0207 ⓦ www.europcar.lt
**Hertz** ⓐ Kalvarijų 14 ⓣ +370 5272 6940 ⓦ www.hertz.lt
**Sixt** ⓐ Rodūnios Kelias 2 (Airport) ⓣ +370 5239 5636 ⓦ www.sixt.lt

The local options are A&A Litinterp and the delightful Rimas Rentacar.

**A&A Litinterp** ⓐ Bernardinų 7-2 ⓣ +370 5212 3850 ⓦ www.litinterp.lt
**Rimas Rentacar** ⓣ +370 5277 6213 ⓔ rimas.cars@is.lt

*St Peter and St Paul's Church is a hidden treasure*

THE CITY OF
Vilnius

REGINA PACIS
FUNDA NOS IN PACE

# Old Town

It won't take you long to see why UNESCO has listed Vilnius Old Town as a World Heritage site, and while that credential doesn't make it unique, the range of architecture on display in Vilnius does. Vilnius has a few hidden artistic treasures that easily rank as the best of their kind in Europe – possibly the world.

Much of Vilnius was shaped by the fact that many different religions and cultures were welcomed here. It was a city of tolerance and acceptance, and the wide range of immigrants all made their particular mark, while Lithuanians also held firmly to and eloquently expressed their culture in the built environment.

## SIGHTS & ATTRACTIONS

### Cathedral

The first Cathedral on this site was erected in 1251 by (minions of) Grand Duke Mindaugas. There were pagan temples prior to that, evidence of which is still visible if you take a tour of the cellars.

This building was designed by Stuoka-Gucevičius from 1769–1820, the architect responsible for parts of the Presidential Palace, and you can see a statue of his stylised head if you walk up the street bearing his name and duck into the little park at the end.

The Cathedral is home to a range of stunning chapels. The most important is St Casimir's, in the northeast corner. St Casimir is the patron saint of Lithuania, and if the image of him in here is anything to go by, he had three hands. Legend has it that the artist who created the picture decided to change the position of the hand, so he painted over it and painted a new hand. The old hand, however, formed a habit of reappearing each time it was painted over. The

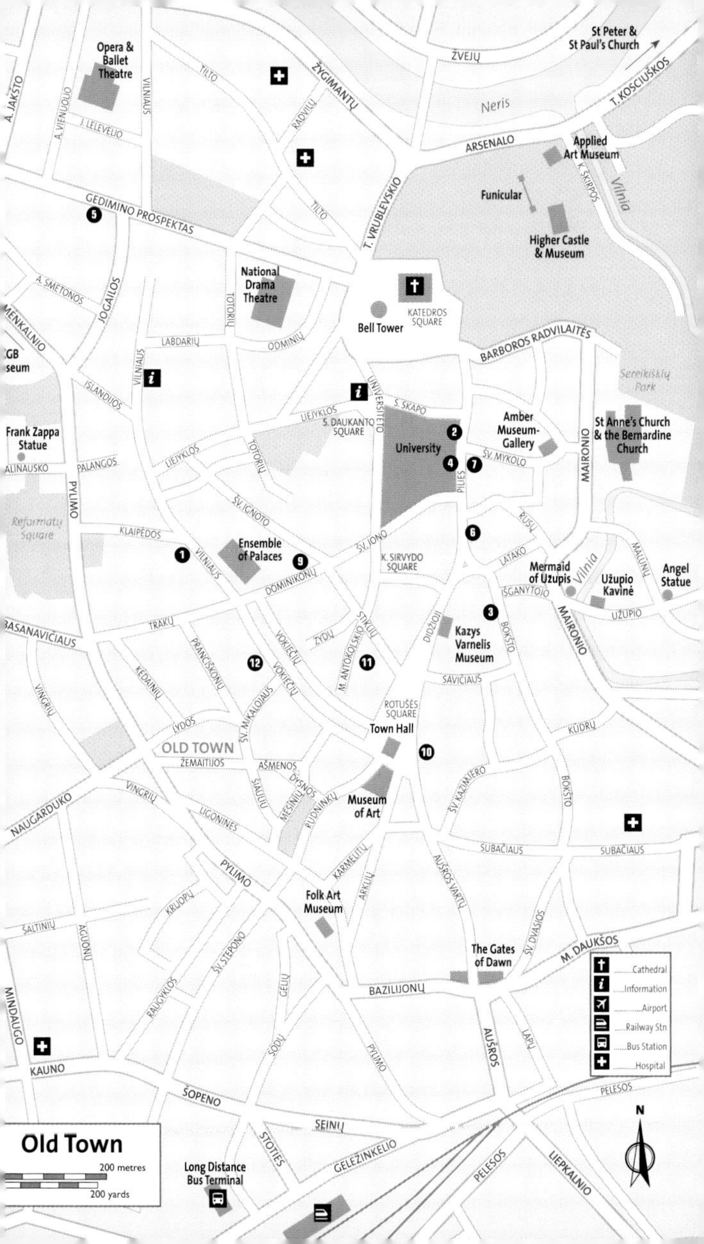
Old Town
200 metres
200 yards
Opera & Ballet Theatre
St Peter & St Paul's Church
ŽVEJŲ
Neris
T. KOSCIUŠKOS
ARSENALO
Applied Art Museum
Funicular
Higher Castle & Museum
K. SKIRPOS
Vilnia
TILTO
ŽYGIMANTŲ
RADVILŲ
A. JAKŠTO
A. VIENUOLIO
J. LELEVELIO
VILNIAUS
GEDIMINO PROSPEKTAS
T. VRUBLEVSKIO
National Drama Theatre
TOTORIŲ
Bell Tower
KATEDROS SQUARE
BARBOROS RADVILAITĖS
A. SMETONOS
JOGAILOS
MENKALNIO
LABDARIŲ
ODMINIŲ
KGB Museum
ISLANDIJOS
UNIVERSITETO
Sereikiškių Park
LIEJYKLOS
S. DAUKANTO SQUARE
S. SKAPO
University
Amber Museum-Gallery
St Anne's Church & the Bernardine Church
Frank Zappa Statue
ŠV. MYKOLO
MAIRONIO
PALANGOS
ALINAUSKO
PILIES
PYLIMO
ŠV. IGNOTO
RUSŲ
Reformatų Square
KLAIPĖDOS
Ensemble of Palaces
ŠV. JONO
K. SIRVYDO SQUARE
LATAKO
MALŪNŲ
Mermaid of Užupis
Užupio Kavinė
Angel Statue
DOMINIKONŲ
IŠGANYTOJO
UŽUPIO
BASANAVIČIAUS
TRAKŲ
DIDŽIOJI
Kazys Varnelis Museum
BOKŠTO
PRANCIŠKONŲ
VOKIEČIŲ
ŽYDŲ
STIKLIŲ
M. ANTOKOLSKIO
KĖDAINIŲ
VINGRIŲ
SAVIČIAUS
ROTUŠĖS SQUARE
Town Hall
ŠV. MIKALOJAUS
LYDOS
OLD TOWN
KŪDRŲ
ŽEMAITIJOS
AŠMENOS
DYSNOS
ŠIAULIŲ
MĖSINIŲ
RUDNINKŲ
Museum of Art
ŠV. KAZIMIERO
NAUGARDUKO
LIGONINĖS
SUBAČIAUS
KARMELITŲ
ARKLIŲ
AUŠROS VARTŲ
Folk Art Museum
KRIJOPU
ŠALTINIŲ
AGUONŲ
ŠV. STEPONO
ŠV. DVASIOS
The Gates of Dawn
M. DAUKŠOS
BAZILIJONŲ
MINDAUGO
RAUGYKLOS
GĖLIŲ
SODŲ
AUŠROS
LAPŲ
Cathedral
Information
Airport
Railway Stn
Bus Station
Hospital
KAUNO
ŠOPENO
PELESOS
SEINŲ
STOTIES
GELEŽINKELIO
N
LIEPKALNIO
Long Distance Bus Terminal

painter eventually concluded that it must be some kind of miracle and left the picture tri-handed.
ⓐ Katedros Square ⓛ 08.00–19.00 daily

**The Gates of Dawn**

In the 16th century, this was the original gate to the city. You had to pay for entry with a rock or stone, thereby making your contribution to the paved streets of the walled city. A chapel was built into the structure above the arched entranceway in 1671 and became a home to a glowing image of the Virgin Mary, which is visible through an open window, and which is supposedly capable of affecting miracles. That's why there are so many little old ladies kneeling in the street before it. The avenue through the archway was, until quite recently, perpetually crowded with vendors selling religious memorabilia and small crowd of beggars. They had a habit of making the short journey through the gates a bit of an unwelcome adventure, but have since been moved on. To really appreciate this cornerstone of Vilnius, duck into a little doorway on your left as you are facing the Virgin Mary, climb the stairs and marvel at the neo-classical interior that was decorated in 1829.
ⓐ Aušros Vartų 12 ⓣ +370 5212 3513

**KGB Museum**

What was formerly both the KGB and Gestapo HQ and prison, and therefore the site of many atrocities, has been turned into a stoic but chilling museum. There's no attempt to glorify or dress up the past, and there doesn't need to be. Simple descriptions on the walls simply state what each room was used for. The water torture room and padded cell are particularly quietening, but the execution chamber takes things to another level again. This is an impressive museum run by volunteers. The no-nonsense set-up they have

created is a totally appropriate and respectable representation of the grisly recent past.

Outside the buildings, names of victims are engraved on the stones in the walls. On weekends, veterans can sometimes be seen gazing mournfully at the names and dates.

This place is not pleasant, but equally not to be missed.
ⓐ Aukų 2a ⓣ +370 5249 6264 ⓗ 10.00–17.00 Tues–Sat, 10.00–15.00 Sundays, closed on Mondays

**St Anne's Church & the Bernardine Church**

There are two different churches crowding each other here. The pretty one closest to the street is St Anne's, an exquisite Gothic building that, legend has it, Napoleon wanted to hold in his hand and carry back to Paris. There are 33 different kinds of decorative bricks used in the construction. The use of bricks, rather than larger blocks, is unique for such a grand church, and gives it a charming hand-made appearance. The church is unimpressive inside, so if you're in a rush, just head past to the church behind it.

This is the Bernardine Church, and quite different to St Anne's in that it's not very pretty on the outside, but hides some treasures inside. Enter through a door at the bottom of the ramp to the right of the main door. Once inside, and as your eyes grow accustomed to the dim light, you'll see some frescoes on the left wall. These are unique in their combination of theme and style. The first – most impressive – one depicts St Christopher carrying a young Jesus across a river. Further into the church, and on the same wall, you will notice some partially revealed confessionals. Behind the wall is a corridor that contains many more frescoes – they were being restored at the time of writing, so it may be worth seeing whether the 'staff only' sign is still on the door. ⓐ Maironio 8

## CULTURE

### Amber Museum-Gallery

Amber is the jewel of the Baltics – except when it contains a dead prehistoric insect, when it just becomes compellingly curious and creepy. The Amber Museum-Gallery is really just a glorified shop, but they have an excellent display downstairs that shows off the main amber discoveries, different types of amber, and some of those inconceivably old inclusions. (Some of them could be a hundred-million years old, and their wings still look crisp.) Also of note is a (fake) presentation of the Juodkrantė Hoard – a famous collection of amber dredged up from the bottom of the Curonian Lagoon by a mining company and, despite the fact that it contains evidence of the lifestyle of Stone Age Baltic tribes, thoughtfully distributed to random and widely scattered recipients as little presents. This is the best amber museum in Lithuania, outside of the coastal town of Palanga.
a Šv. Mykolo 8 t +370 5262 3092 10.00–19.00

### The Applied Art Museum

While Vilnius's Royal Palace is being reconstructed behind the Cathedral, remnants of the original can be found here. What may at first look like a collection of bits of rubble takes on new meaning when you discover something of its context, and then glance at the rapidly growing reconstruction site. There's also a fragment of the former city wall still visible in the basement. Of course, being an art museum, you will also find plenty of art, most of it both very old (from the 16th century) and much of it with a religious flavour. This can be a bit of a serious place, and cameras and rampaging children with ice creams and sticky fingers are not welcomed. (Well-behaved children are, of course, quite welcome.)

Arsenalo 3a 11.00–17.30, 11.00–15.30 Sundays, closed on Mondays

**Higher Castle**

This is really just a modest tower, but it is as iconic of Vilnius as anything, and climbing to the top is a must even if you don't care too much for the modest museum that you'll pass through on the way. The view from the top is worth the climb, not just as you can see such a bizarre jumble of roofs, but also because you can see the layout of the city that you just couldn't manage otherwise. Bring binoculars and a camera with a decent zoom if you have them.

*The Amber Museum-Gallery features some excellent displays*

**Higher Castle Museum**

The museum itself contains some old medieval decoration and artefacts, but what is most interesting is the model of how the whole castle complex looked before it was reduced to, well... the single tower that you're now visiting.

ⓐ Castle Hill, Arsenalo 5 ⓣ +370 5261 7453 ◷ 10.00–17.00, closed Mondays

**Kazys Varnelis Museum**

Kazys Varnelis is a Lithuanian artist who spent a large chunk of time in the USA after escaping the Soviet occupation in 1949. He did quite well in the land of stars and stripes, creating pattern-based optical illusion stuff, but done on a large scale. In addition to creating such op-art pieces, he also collected a magnificent hoard of art and furniture covering a broad range of periods, cultures and styles.

He returned to Lithuania in 1998 and, thankfully, brought his collection with him. You can now visit it here. Everything has been scattered carefully about 33 rooms by Varnelis himself who, unlike some curator with a dusty old degree, isn't afraid to chuck a bit of Pop Art in with a baroque suite.

ⓐ Didžioji 26 ⓣ +370 5279 1644 ◷ 09.00–17.00, closed Sun & Mon

ⓘ Appointments are necessary

## RETAIL THERAPY

Pilies Street is packed with tourist shops, both ramshackle street-side affairs staffed by ex-bag ladies, and ones with floors and doors and nicely dressed staff who speak perfect English. Here you can buy amber and linen, among other bits and pieces like t-shirts with the hammer-and-sickle logo, little flags, fridge magnets and other blah. At the point where Pilies Street becomes Didžioji Street, there is a little market with stalls selling more of the same on one side of the road, and artwork on the other side. There are plans to move this market to an area just off the eastern edge of the Old Town map – the intersection of Maironio and Aukštaičių streets, so if they do move it, you know where to go looking for it.

When buying amber, be careful that you're not actually buying toffee. Mosaics made of hundreds of little chips of 'amber' have been known to melt and dribble down the wall when hung in direct sunlight – and that's because they're not made of amber at all, they're made of sugar. You can test amber by either eating it (if it's sweet and melts in your mouth, or tastes like plastic, it's fake) or burning it (if it smells like pine-scented toilet freshener, it's real), but most sellers won't let you try either method. Sugar can be discreetly spotted with a damp finger, but a good guide is the price – you get what you pay for. Another clue: the shops with doors are generally reliable, authoritative, and not in the business of selling sugar.

## TAKING A BREAK

**Balti Drambliai** £ ❶ We list this one because it's the only non-smoking and vegetarian place. They have a pleasant courtyard in summer, but otherwise you'll have to burrow into the basement. ⓐ Vilniaus 41 ⓣ +370 5262 0875 ⓛ 11.00–24.00, except on weekends when they open from 12.00

**Čili Kava** £ ❷ This is the place to head for if you want to order at the counter and carry your coffee and cake to the table on a plastic tray. And then come back because you forgot to pick up sugar or something. It's cheap. ⓐ Pilies 16 ⓣ +370 5260 9028

07.30–22.00 Mon–Thur, 07.30–23.00 Fri, 09.00–23.00 Sat, 09.00–22.00 Sun

**Mano Kavinė £ 3** A hidden favourite for locals who like the laid-back atmosphere, cheap eats, aquarium and free use of the internet on the computer at the bar. There's a bit of a slack charm here, and it's also worth noting that it springs to life in the evenings. a Bokšto 7 t +370 5215 3000 11.00–02.00 Mon–Thur, open until 04.00 Fri & Sat, and 01.00 Sun w www.manokavine.lt

**Pilies Kepyklėlė £ 4** A charming café, littered with doilies and cream cakes and little old ladies stuffing their faces. The salads, crêpes and some of the pasta dishes are excellent, as is the location. It's not worth going out of your way for, but considering that it's probably on your way, you'll probably end up in here anyway. There are two types of cake here that are worth trying if they have them: *Medaus Tortas* is a layered honey cake, which is delicious, while *Tinginys* ('lazybones' cake) is a biscuity-fudgey concoction that has the appearance, consistency and digestibility of brown concrete. a Pilies 19 t +370 5260 8992 09.00–23.00

**Pizza Jazz £ 5** Somehow this chain of restaurants has managed to get 'pizza' and 'classy' to mean something other than the complete opposite of each other – especially at their Gedimino restaurant, where you can sip white wine or a cool beer while watching the people promenade past the window. a Gedimino 20 t +370 5212 0839 10.00–24.00 w www.pizzajazz.lt

*Take a stroll through the town*

**Double Coffee £–££** ❻ It's a chain-style place (with outlets across the Baltic states), but actually serves extremely good tea and coffee and a good range of salads, light meals, sweets and snacks. It's overpriced by local standards, but the only place to get some of the more interesting varieties of coffee, tea and other concoctions. They have two locations in Old Town, both of which are great for people-watching if you can get a street-side table. ⓐ Pilies 34 ⓣ +370 6503 7634 ⓐ Gedimino 26 ⓣ +370 5261 4175 ⓐ Gedimino 5 ⓣ +370 5261 4723 ⓦ www.doublecoffee.lt

**Sereikiškių Park** A walk along the river through this park is a pleasure that can easily be squeezed into a busy day, as the park is right in the middle of everything. There are a couple of places where you can sit on the bank under the shade of a tree and just listen to the music of the river flowing by. In the daytime, you'll often see couples, students with books, and young families. By early evening, they will have left and been replaced by 'yoofs' drinking beer from plastic bottles, which will give you the opportunity to note that black leather, chains and big safety pins are still popular here.

If you're entering the park from the Cathedral Square, look for the ice-cream stands behind the Cathedral itself.

## AFTER DARK

### Restaurants

**Forto Dvaras £** ❼ They serve the best *cepelinai* in town – simple as that. Countless varieties of Lithuania's favourite national dish are available here, as are more standard international offerings of the piece-of-meat-and-veggies type. The interior is a bit McTwee but still quite pleasant. There's a country-home theme upstairs, cellars downstairs, and tables that spill onto the gorgeous 'Castle Street' in summer. ⓐ Pilies 16 ⓣ +370 5261 1070 ⓛ 11.00–24.00

**Čingino ££** ❽ Drop in here for a Russian-style evening of food, vodka, more food, bad music and loud laughter. It's a stylish brick-vaulted cellar with a tiled floor and can become very noisy when full of people having a good time. Food, however, is both flavoursome and very, very filling. You might be tempted to splash out on Russian vodka while you're here, but it's really not necessary, as Lithuanian vodka is much cheaper, and generally just as good. ⓐ Basanavičiaus 11 ⓣ +370 5261 5555 ⓛ 12.00–24.00

**Cozy ££** ❾ The cruisy café that sets the standard and attracts plenty of groovy young things who don't mind paying too much to eat too little. The smooth, slack style is what it's all about, but the fact that the snacks and light meals on offer are also of a very high standard doesn't hurt. On weekend evenings, there's a DJ-bar cave-lounge space that always attracts more people than it can comfortably accommodate. ⓐ Dominikonų 10 ⓣ +370 5261 1137 ⓦ www.cozy.lt ⓛ 09.00–01.00, except weekend evenings until 06.00 and Sun until 01.00

**Helios ££–£££** ❿ The Helios centre, right next to the town hall, contains a nightclub, steak restaurant, Japanese restaurant, casino and sports bar. All of them are excellent, although completely lacking any theme or decoration that might be construed as even slightly Lithuanian. The nightclub is extremely modern and popular, while the restaurants are among the best, with a few offering each particular type of cuisine. ⓐ Didžioji 28 ⓛ Each venue keeps its own hours, but the centre is almost always open

**Lokys £££** ⓫ One of Vilnius's oldest, most respected restaurants, famous for offering hunters' delights such as beaver as well as traditional Lithuanian dishes, has expanded to include a modern steak restaurant. Actually getting into the place can be an adventure in itself, as the cellars are accessed via a very narrow twisting stairway. Once you're down there you can choose from various nooks, halls, and little rooms, one of which used to be a prison cell. Wherever you choose to eat it, the food is first class, and on weekend evenings served with Medieval themed music and entertainment. Ideal for group parties. ⓐ Stiklių 8 ⓣ +370 5262 9046 ⓦ www.lokys.lt ⓛ 12.00–24.00

**Žemaičiai £££** ⓬ For a bit of an authentic adventure and some traditional food, this one is hard to beat. The food is mostly good, but they just can't manage consistency for some reason, despite ambitious prices. Still, the rabbit-warren interior is worthwhile. When you enter, walk straight past the vacant bar and head downstairs, taking care not to bang your head on the low ceiling on the way. ⓐ Vokiečių 24 ⓣ +370 5261 6573 ⓦ www.zemaiciai.lt ⓛ 11.00–24.00

**Bars & Clubs**

**Aukštaičiai** Somewhat hidden in a quaint little street that goes to nowhere, this place has become a popular haunt for locals and expats who are after good times in an easy-going venue that can also turn on half-decent Lithuanian food if required. There are three main areas so groups can be accommodated without clearing the place out. It is also known for longevity – the parties here often continue well past sunrise. ⓐ Antokolskio 13 ⓣ +370 5212 0169 ⓦ www.aukstaiciai.lt ⓛ 08.00–04.00

**Briusly** Pronounced 'Bruce Lee', and inspired by his films that were a black-market hit in the Soviet days. The owners say they want to break traditions and apply a fresh approach – Bruce Lee-style – but it just doesn't matter what they say because the fact that the place is packed with fresh-faced happy people having a good time every

*Mixing it in one of Vilnius's many night spots*

night of the week speaks for itself. ⓐ Šv Ignoto 12 ⓣ +370 6741 1059 ⓗ 07.00–24.00, except Thur–Sat when they stay open until 02.00

**Brodvėjus** They've got creating a raw appeal down to a fine art, and everyone goes there because everyone else goes there. Actually, every city in Eastern Europe has a place not unlike this, where they play dodgy music, and balding old foreign men dance with pretty young girls.

In any case, it's one of a few places that are open every night of the week, and can be relied upon for providing a fun and friendly atmosphere at any time. There's a large barn-style area downstairs shared between a gaggle of tables and chairs, and a modest dance floor. Overlooking this is a balcony, also decked out with tables and chairs, which is the perfect spot for those who are more into people-watching than participating. There's also a lively bar in another room downstairs, and a lounge-style room upstairs. The mix of cacophonous and crazy on the one hand and a bit more laid-back and mellow on the other is ideal, and part of the simple yet successful recipe that ensures this place is always cooking. Oh yes – and meals are available at all times too. ⓐ Mėsinių 4 ⓣ +370 5210 7208 ⓦ www.brodvejus.lt ⓗ 12.00–02.00 Sun, 12.00–03.00 Mon, 12.00–04.00 Tues, 12.00–05.00 all other days

**Connect** Notable for having a huge dancing space and a massive screen and audiovisual system, this club attracts a younger tracksuit-and-sunglasses-wearing and glowing-stick-waving crowd, who like to do something that is not so much dancing, but more like directing imaginary traffic. It's a well set-up space in a great location and worth burrowing into (yes, it's a basement affair). ⓐ Vokiečių 2 ⓣ +370 5212 2031 ⓦ www.connectclub.lt ⓗ 22.00–05.00 Wed–Sat

**Fashion Club** The Fashion TV franchise was always bound to be a success in Lithuania as there are plenty of pretty, aspirational and style-conscious glamourpusses keen to strut their stuff, and no shortage of rich foreigners (often Russians) who wish to buy them drinks. Regardless of whether you think it's sensational or shallow, you'd have to agree the place is well set up and has a great techno-cave type of atmosphere. Watch the glossy tile dance floor when they start spraying bubbles around – it gets slippery. ⓐ Trakų 2 ⓣ +370 5243 0777 ⓦ www.ftv.lt ◷ Thur–Sat 21.00–06.00

**Gras'as** Weird in a friendly and efficient kind of way, and bristling with grass. There's grass on the ceiling, in the toilets, and even on the lampshades. Food is decent pub-grub quality, making this a good choice for either a casual meal or a drink with friends. If the live jazz kills your conversation, be aware that there are several rooms to either side that may be a bit quieter. You can also sit street-side upstairs and be looked at by everyone who passes by while a garden gnome holds up your table. ⓐ Vokiečių 2 ⓣ +370 5212 2031 ⓦ www.grasas.lt ◷ 11.00–24.00 Mon & Tues, 11.00–02.00 Wed & Thur, 11.00–03.00 Fri & Sat, 12.00–24.00 Sun

**Iki Aušros** This cocktail bar is as smooth as a Slippery Nipple and staffed by the sort of shakers who know the difference between a Classic Martini, a Vodka Martini, a Bradford, and an idiot who thinks he's James Bond. It's frequented by a gently elite set of locals and expats. ⓐ Aušros Vartų 15 ⓣ +370 6100 4131 ◷ 19.00–02.00, but stays open until 04.00 Fri & Sat

**Lithuanian Wild Club** This place has a long history of being attended by skinheads who would be dangerous if they weren't so mentally challenged. Now, however, a new door policy is turning them away. The general tidy-up also affected the music and lighting, and the staff, who have pretty new costumes to wear. Note that there is constant topless dancing – it's still that kind of place. It's unsophisticated, but safe, well run, and fun. There's also a bit of a naughty room out the back for those who are basically looking for a full-strength strip show. ⓐ Gedimino 24 ⓣ +370 5262 4473 ⓦ www.wild.lt ⓛ 21.00–06.00, although they do shut earlier when there's not much happening

**Pabo Latino** Whether you actually want to dance Latino, or just swish around looking cool or watching other people looking cool, this is the place to come. It's a top-class club with exquisite decoration, a classy clientele, and lots of people queuing at the door in order to either pay a small fortune to get in, or get turned away by face control. In summer, a courtyard is decked out (literally) to allow outdoor dancing, and lounging about under tents. It can be a pit of pretentious suits and blondes at the weekends, but keep in mind that Wednesday and Thursday nights are a bit more casual, and cheaper. ⓐ Trakų 3/2 ⓣ +370 5262 1045 ⓦ www.pabolatino.lt ⓛ 20.00–01.00 Wed, 20.00–03.00 Thur, 20.00–05.00 Fri & Sat

**Prospekto Pubas** What looks pretty uninteresting by day goes completely crazy at night and becomes one of the city's hottest clubs, catering for frivolous students and the sorts of tourists who chase them and their rhythmically wiggling bottoms. Make of that what you will, but rest assured that the crowd, music and atmosphere here usually can be relied upon for a good night out. It tends to stay open until 06.00 on weekend evenings, which is a little later than most other clubs, so it's a good one to put on the list as your second option if you like to visit a few venues in one night. ⓐ Gedimino 2 ⓣ +370 5212 0832 ⓗ 11.00–05.00

**Savas Kampas** The no-theme, no-pressure, no-fuss and no-chance-of-a-good-meal option for catching up with friends and enjoying a drink and a snack. The two rooms at the back are pleasant, with plenty of comfortable couches, but can be a bit dark and dingy. Service is pretty poor, so don't be afraid to get up and chase a waiter or waitress if you need to. ⓐ Vokiečių 4 ⓣ +370 5212 3203 ⓦ www.savaskampas.lt ⓗ 09.00–01.00 Mon–Wed, 09.00–02.00 Thur, 09.00–04.00 Fri, 10.00–04.00 Sat, 10.00–01.00 Sun

**ŠMC** 'ŠMC' stands for Contemporary Art Centre in Lithuanian, so it's hardly surprising that this place, despite its tired old furniture and dingy atmosphere, is perpetually jam-packed with morose twittering poets, exuberant artists, and a couple of crusty old characters who seem to have started a game of chess here in the Soviet times and still haven't finished (maybe they both think it's the other guy's turn to move). Fun if you can get into it. ⓐ Vokiečių 2 ⓣ +370 5261 7097 ⓗ 11.00–24.00 Mon–Thur, until 03.00 Fri, 12.00–01.00 Sat, 12.00–24.00 Sun

# Užupis & Belmontas

The Užupis district is often described as having an alternative and arty aspect to it – something like Montmartre in Paris, Soho in London or Greenwich Village in New York. The reputation has probably been created by travel writers looking for a headline, but is not really deserved. While Užupis is indeed delightful, it doesn't actually have any more to offer in terms of art and culture than the Old Town. The charm of the area comes not from cafés, museums and galleries, but from the crumbling old buildings, a café (the only place in Vilnius where you can have a beer by the river) and an angel.

There is indeed an alternative aspect to the region, which has half-mockingly declared itself an independent republic and has its own constitution, but most of the time it's just asleep. If you're after anything more interesting than a quiet stroll, the best time to visit Užupis is on the first day of April, when the 'republic' celebrates its independence, will stamp your passport on entry, and entertain you with all manner of nonsense for the day.

Užupis is, if anything, misunderstood. Best to visit with an open mind, and always open eyes.

## SIGHTS & ATTRACTIONS

### Bernardinų Cemetery

This is really the only cemetery that is within walking distance of the centre, and is worth a visit for those who, for whatever reason, like visiting cemeteries. It was established in 1820, and the little chapel near the entrance was built some 18 years later. Had they realised at that time that the hill on which it is located would slowly

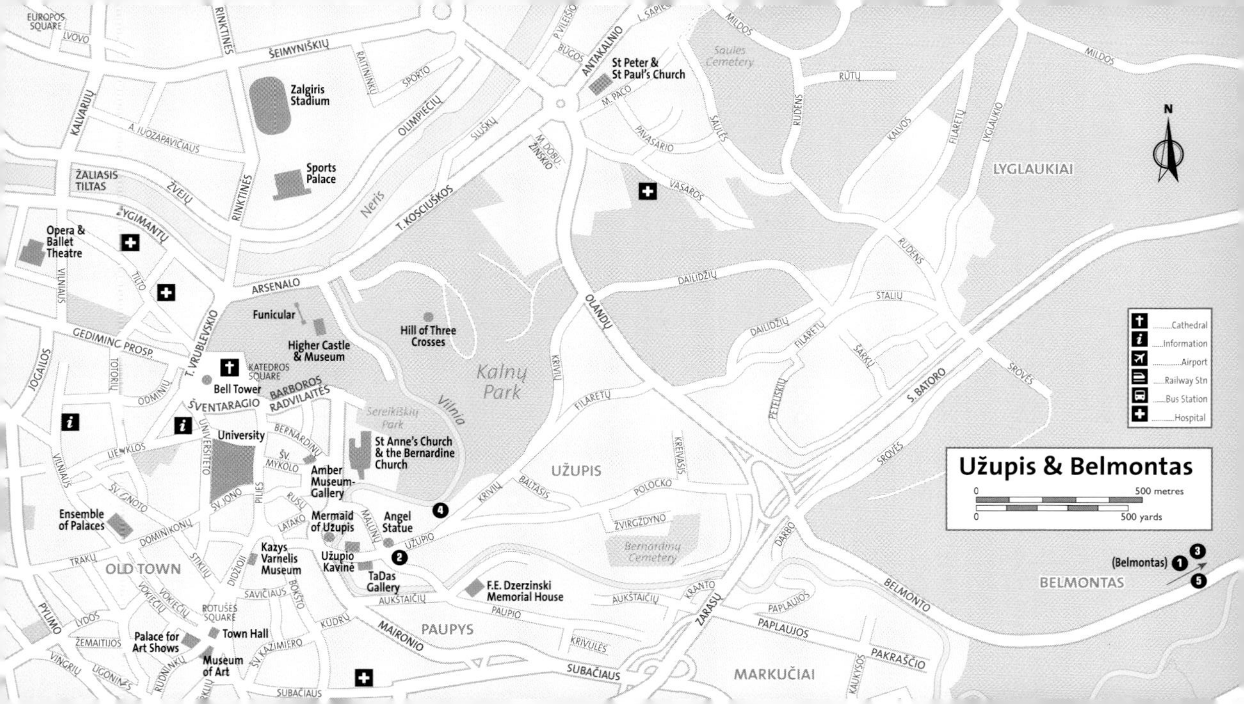

Užupis & Belmontas
0
500 metres
0
500 yards
Cathedral
Information
Airport
Railway Stn
Bus Station
Hospital
N
LYGLAUKIAI
UŽUPIS
BELMONTAS
MARKUČIAI
PAUPYS
OLD TOWN
(Belmontas)
St Peter & St Paul's Church
Saulės Cemetery
Zalgiris Stadium
Sports Palace
Opera & Ballet Theatre
Funicular
Higher Castle & Museum
Hill of Three Crosses
Kalnų Park
Vilnia
Neris
Sereikiškių Park
St Anne's Church & the Bernardine Church
Amber Museum-Gallery
Mermaid of Užupis
Angel Statue
Užupio Kavinė
TaDas Gallery
F.E. Dzerzinski Memorial House
Bernardinų Cemetery
Kazys Varnelis Museum
Town Hall
Museum of Art
Palace for Art Shows
Ensemble of Palaces
University
Bell Tower
KATEDROS SQUARE
ROTUŠĖS SQUARE
EUROPOS SQUARE
ŽALIASIS TILTAS
GEDIMINO PROSP.
T. VRUBLEVSKIO
T. KOSCIUŠKOS
ARSENALO
ŠVENTARAGIO
BARBOROS RADVILAITĖS
OLANDŲ
S. BATORO
BELMONTO
ZARASŲ
MAIRONIO
SUBAČIAUS
PAPLAUJOS
PAKRAŠČIO
KAUKYSOS
MILDOS
RŪTŲ
RUDENS
KALVOS
FILARETŲ
LYGLAUKIO
SRAVĖS
SROVĖS
STALIŲ
DAILIDŽIŲ
ŠARKŲ
PETEUSKIŲ
DARBO
KRIVIŲ
KREIVASIS
POLOCKO
BALTASIS
ŽVIRGŽDYNO
UŽUPIO
MALŪNŲ
AUKŠTAIČIŲ
KRANTO
PAPLAUJOS
PAUPIO
KRIVULĖS
KŪDRŲ
SV. KAZIMIERO
BOKŠTO
SAVIČIAUS
DIDŽIOJI
STIKLIŲ
DOMINIKONŲ
ŠV. JONO
PILIES
UNIVERSITETO
ŠV. MYKOLO
BERNARDINŲ
RUSŲ
LATAKO
ŠV. IGNOTO
LIEJYKLOS
VILNIAUS
TRAKŲ
VOKIEČIŲ
LYDOS
PYLIMO
ŽEMAITIJOS
VINGRIŲ
UGONINĖS
RŪDNINKŲ
TOTORIŲ
ODMINIŲ
JOGAILOS
TILTO
ŽYGIMANTŲ
ŽVEJŲ
RINKTINĖS
A. JUOZAPAVIČIAUS
KALVARIJŲ
LVOVO
ŠEIMYNIŠKIŲ
RAITININKŲ
SPORTO
OLIMPIEČIŲ
SLUŠKŲ
M. DOBUŽINSKIO
ANTAKALNIO
BUGOS
P. VILEIŠIO
L. SAPIEGOS
M. PACO
PAVASARIO
SAULĖS
VASAROS

erode into the river below, they would have chosen another location. Some who were placed here for eternal rest have found the ground falling away beneath them. Buried here are university professors, scientists, artists and other intellectuals. You will notice that there are many Polish-sounding names on the tombstones. It's a beautiful place to visit in autumn and winter, when the ramshackle grounds and graves clinging to the eroding hillside are sprinkled with either golden leaves or snow. ⓐ Žvirgždyno 3

**Constitution**

As the Užupis area is something of a self-declared breakaway republic, they have their own constitution. You can find the full text of the constitution on a large plaque, proudly displayed on one of the walls that isn't crumbling, just a short wander down Paupio, heading away from the angel. The constitution declares, among other things, that:

People have the right to die, but it's not a duty.
People have the right to be insignificant and unknown.
A dog has the right to be a dog.
People have the right to be misunderstood.

**Crumbling walls**

The term 'delightfully decrepit' has often been used to describe the buildings in Užupis. Everything seems age-worn and weather-beaten, and photographers in particular love wandering around, looking for that rich-with-character shot.

**Graffiti**

Can you find the cartoon snail? Or what about the sign that says 'sky (*dangus*) – 12km' under an arrow that points straight up?

Whether it be stencilled, hand sprayed, or simply scrawled, the smattering of graffiti on the crumbling walls of Užupis adds a certain character to the area. There is no one particular destination to head for if you are a fan of graffiti, it's just a case of taking note of it as you wander around.

**Hill of Three Crosses**

Arguably, this isn't actually in Užupis, but it's on the same side of the river and you can reach it from Užupis (via Kalnų Parkas) so we'll mention it here. The three white crosses atop this hill are visible from many locations in Vilnius Old Town and are somewhat iconic of the city. One story behind it suggests that seven Franciscan monks were killed here by pagans who tied them to their crosses, then threw them down the hill and into the river. Another less interesting version of events is that the crosses were erected to commemorate Vilnius being granted the Magdeburg Rights (basically, rights to be a city), as was done in many other cities. However they got there, Stalin didn't think much of the crosses, so they were torn down and buried. You can see some of the wreckage of the former crosses as you climb up to see the shiny new ones, and admire a great view of the city.

**St Peter & St Paul's Church**

It's a trolleybus journey or twenty-minute walk out of town, but worth it. While it's not much to look at from the outside, the church is home to a couple of thousand gently cavorting characters – plaster stuccoes clinging to the walls and dripping from the ceilings. It's easily one of Vilnius's hidden treasures. It was commissioned in 1668 and a team of Italians worked their baroque magic until the money ran out. Hence, the area around the altar is a bit plain in

comparison to the rest of the interior. You'll also notice a chandelier ship floating overhead while you're in here, made from brass and a very impressive collection of clear glass marbles. It is a relatively recent addition to the church, being made in Latvia in 1905.
ⓐ Antakalnio 1 ⓣ +370 5234 0229 Trolleybus: 2, 3, 4, 14 or 17, from the stop opposite the bridge that crosses the river nearest to the Cathedral, heading east

**Užupis Angel & Mermaid**

The most prominent feature of Užupis is an angel on a stick. The statue of the angel that you can now see was unveiled on 1 April 2001, and now not only balances on a golden ball, but blows a trumpet across the rooftops. It's certainly one of Vilnius's most amusing and pleasing sculptures, as all the others seem to be a bit stern and severe. The effeminate and flighty angel is a breath of fresh air. Before the angel, the plinth on top of the stick was adorned with a big egg. So, it's fair to say that the angel hatched out of an egg. The egg in question was sold in an auction and now stands atop another big stick in the Jewish district (near the corner of Pylimo and Raugyklos streets).

The other notable statue in Užupis is the Mermaid of Užupis (*Užupio Mergelė*), set into a little cove in the wall of the river opposite the Užupio Kavinė. We're not sure exactly what the mermaid is supposed to mean, but she certainly means something to the residents because when she mysteriously disappeared one morning they were all a bit concerned. It turned out that ice forming around her bottom had squeezed her out of place and dumped her into, or rather onto, the frozen river, where she was

*Vision of an angel*

carried some way with the ice floes. She also took a dip when the river swelled during flooding in 2005.

**Walks**

You can walk from the Užupis area to the Kalnų Park and the Hill of Three Crosses, into Sereikiškių Park, and also to the Saints Peter's and Paul's Church. If you're keen for a longer stroll, you can head out to Belmontas. We suggest investing in a detailed map if you want to explore the paths in the parks here.

## CULTURE

If you start from the bridge where Užupio crosses the river, walk either over or under the outdoor seating deck of Užupio Kavinė, and then follow the river where you will pass some interesting artists' workshops. Some of the artwork – mainly sculpture – can be seen placed outside along the river. Last time we checked, we saw what looked like a cross between a rock and a washing machine. The workshops here (and we use that term generously) are a bit bohemian and therefore have opening hours along the 'when we feel like it, man' lines – take a chance if you have time on your hands.

**Tadas Gallery**

Tadas Gutauskas, who likes his name to be written 'TaDas', just so you know he is one of those arty types for whom one capital letter just isn't enough, is a prolific Vilnius-born artist who churns out sculptures, paintings and textiles. You can visit his gallery space and browse his creations that range from simply refreshing and innocently fun to

*One of the many orthodox churches in Vilnius*

cringe-worthy kitsch. There are no regular opening hours, so you'll have to call in advance to see when it might be okay to drop in.
ⓐ Užupio 3–5 ⓣ +370 5215 4550 ⓦ www.tadasgutauskas.lt

## RETAIL THERAPY

There isn't any. Being of the new age, alternative, poetry-scribbling and capitalist-scorning types, people in Užupis have no need for shops other than those that sell cheese, lentils, beads and second-hand clothes. We did notice one or two highbrow shops selling expensive interior decoration knick-knacks that rich people will scatter around their expensive apartments, but cannot be sure that they will still be there by the time we go to print, so we won't list them. If they are still there, you'll find them easily.

## TAKING A BREAK

**Belmontas** ❶ What was once a water mill with a bit of a shady inn operating on the side has now become a huge complex of restaurants and areas for relaxation. At the time of writing, there were three restaurants here (including Joana Carinova Tavern and Villa Gloria, listed on pages 88–9), and plans for more. It feels like there are more than that, as each of the restaurants has different areas with different styles. Even if you don't fancy a meal, walking around the pleasant surroundings is a treat as you cannot only explore the water mill itself, but also take a walk through the Pavilniai Regional Park.

Belmontas is a good 40-minute walk from Užupis, most of it along the side of a narrow road. Taking a taxi is recommended – it should cost no more than 15 or 20 litas.

**Prie Angelo £** ❷ The cool little café right beside the angel is clean and fresh but still has a bit of an alternative feel to it. The furniture is wrought-iron artwork (with cushions to make your bottom happy) and there are a few angels stuccoed to the walls here and there. In an effort not to be too original, they serve pizzas, but there are also other more pleasing options on the menu. ⓐ Užupio 9 ⓣ +370 5215 3790 ⓛ 09.00–23.00, 09.00–24.00 Fri & Sat

## AFTER DARK

**Joana Carinova Tavern ££** ❸ Traditional Lithuanian meals are available in the impressive Belmontas complex in this barmy barn that is bristling with stuffed animals' heads and antlers. At the weekends, there is a more feminine hall available upstairs, but regardless of where you eat or what you make of the hacked-from-a-log interior, the food is excellent. ⓐ Belmonto 17 ⓣ +370 6861 4656 ⓦ www.belmontas.lt ⓛ 12.00–23.00, 12.00–24.00 Fri & Sat

**Tores ££** ❹ There is only one venue of interest in Užupis after the sun goes down – Tores. This restaurant has the best view in Vilnius as it is nestled on a hill that overlooks Old Town. Unfortunately, however, the food is mediocre and overpriced. Inside and downstairs is a small wine cellar and art gallery where you can also dine in cooler weather. ⓐ Užupio 40 ⓣ +370 5262 9309 ⓦ www.tores.lt

**Villa Gloria £££** ❺ This is the posh restaurant in the Belmontas complex, and the ideal venue if you want to splash out – not least because it has a little swimming pool in the middle of the dining room. The wine list is outstanding, but so are some of the prices. ⓐ Belmonto 17 ⓣ +370 6152 0220 ⓦ www.belmontas.lt ⓛ 12.00–24.00

# Central & New Vilnius

Outside of the Old Town, Vilnius loses much of its charm but none of its interest. You'll see everything from gleaming glass office towers to some still raw and ugly outcrops of the Soviet era. You can dine in exquisite and refined luxury, or watch people pushing around wobbly-wheeled shopping trolleys overflowing with carcasses at the market. It's where things can take on a decidedly gritty and bizarre edge. It feels coarse and real. Because it is.

## SIGHTS & ATTRACTIONS

### Church of St Michael & St Konstantine

This orthodox church is most notable for the enormous green onions that stand out so garishly against a blue sky (when there is one) and explain why architects probably shouldn't allow their four-year-old children to choose colour schemes. Actually, details on why the roof is such a vibrant shade of green are strangely unavailable.
ⓐ Basanavičiaus 27

### Frank Zappa Statue

One of the more obvious symbols of Vilnius's weirdness is the head of Frank Zappa mounted on a post. The head just sits there doing nothing, which is appropriate because Frank Zappa has nothing to do with Vilnius whatsoever. In a way, his irrelevance makes him a most relevant choice for a random statue. The more peculiar something is, the more appropriate it is as a symbol of Vilnius, and Mr Zappa was quite peculiar. The Zappa likeness was, not surprisingly, commissioned by students, who convinced authorities to allow it to be erected in 1995 by arguing that Mr Zappa looked a

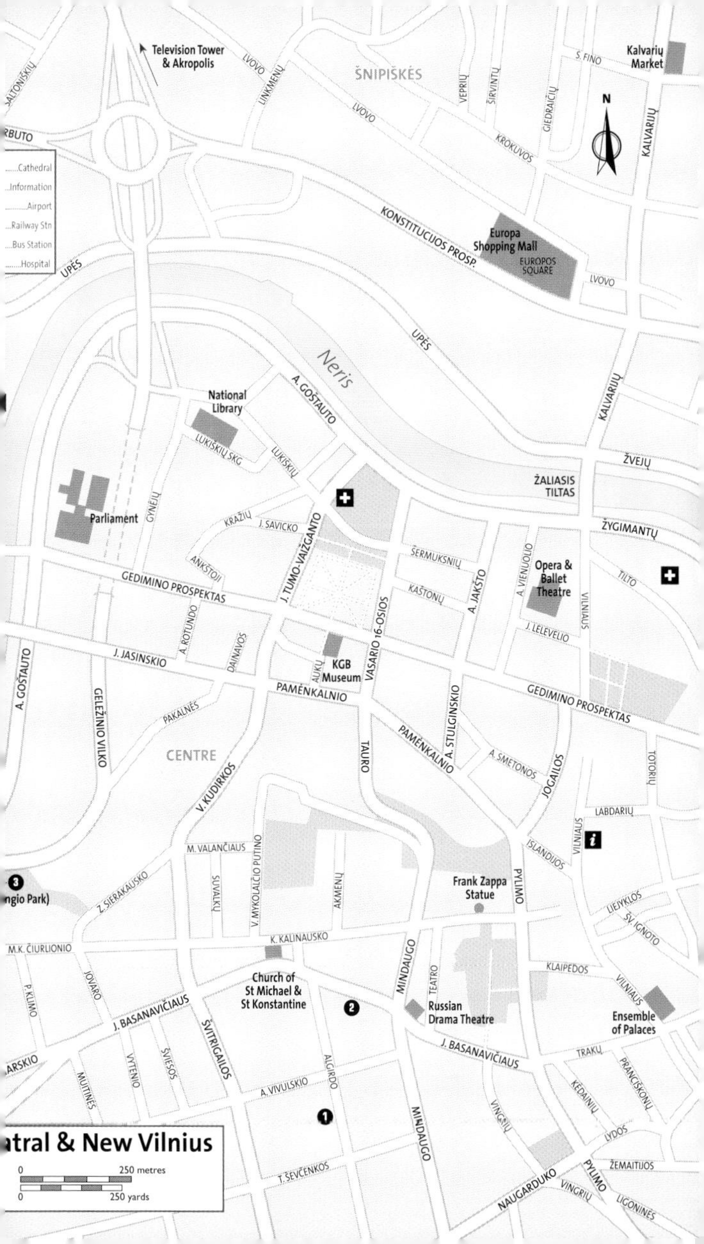

Television Tower & Akropolis
ŠNIPIŠKĖS
Kalvarių Market
Cathedral
Information
Airport
Railway Stn
Bus Station
Hospital
Europa Shopping Mall
EUROPOS SQUARE
KONSTITUCIJOS PROSP.
Neris
National Library
Parliament
ŽALIASIS TILTAS
Opera & Ballet Theatre
GEDIMINO PROSPEKTAS
KGB Museum
CENTRE
Frank Zappa Statue
Church of St Michael & St Konstantine
Russian Drama Theatre
Ensemble of Palaces
ngio Park)
atral & New Vilnius
0
250 metres
0
250 yards
LVOVO
LINKMENŲ
VEPRIŲ
ŠIRVINTŲ
GIEDRAIČIŲ
Š. FINO
KROKUVOS
KALVARIŲ
UPĖS
A. GOŠTAUTO
LUKIŠKIŲ SKG
LUKIŠKIŲ
GYNĖJŲ
KRAŽIŲ
J. SAVICKO
J. TUMO-VAIŽGANTO
ŠERMUKSNIŲ
KAŠTONŲ
A. JAKŠTO
A. VIENUOLIO
ŽVEJŲ
ŽYGIMANTŲ
TILTO
VILNIAUS
J. LELEVELIO
ANKŠTOJI
A. ROTUNDO
DAINAVOS
J. JASINSKIO
AUKŲ
VASARIO 16-OSIOS
PAMĖNKALNIO
GELEŽINIO VILKO
PAKALNĖS
TAURO
A. STULGINSKIO
A. SMETONOS
JOGAILOS
TOTORIŲ
LABDARIŲ
V. KUDIRKOS
M. VALANČIAUS
ISLANDIJOS
PYLIMO
Z. SIERAKAUSKO
SUVALKŲ
V. MYKOLAIČIO PUTINO
AKMENŲ
LIEJYKLOS
ŠV. IGNOTO
M.K. ČIURLIONIO
K. KALINAUSKO
MINDAUGO
TEATRO
KLAIPĖDOS
P. KLIMO
JOVARO
J. BASANAVIČIAUS
ŠVITRIGAILOS
VYTENIO
ŠVIESOS
MUITINĖS
ARSKIO
ALGIRDO
A. VIVULSKIO
TRAKŲ
PRANCIŠKONŲ
KĖDAINIŲ
VINGRIŲ
LYDOS
ŽEMAITIJOS
T. ŠEVČENKOS
NAUGARDUKO
LIGONINĖS
RBUTO
SALTONIŠKIŲ

bit Jewish. Once given the nod, the sculpture was created by Konstantinas Bogdanas, who had previously honed his sculpting skills on the head of Lenin in Moscow.

ⓐ Kalinausko 1

**Parliament**

While the parliament buildings are not much to look at – they're kind of boxy and boring – there are some ugly but interesting blocks of concrete assembled to form a bit of a monument to the west side of the building. They are worth a quick peek if you're in the area. These blocks were part of a barrier that was used to defend the parliament building against Soviet tanks in January 1991, which were trying to storm it.

ⓐ Gedimino 53

**Television Tower**

The Vilnius TV Tower is the tallest building in Lithuania, and, at 326 m (1,070 ft), is a couple of metres taller than the Eiffel tower. (That comparison includes the aerial bit on top of both structures.) It offers great views from a gently revolving restaurant. That, however, is not the reason to go there, for on 13 January 1991 the TV Tower pretty much punctured history when it became the centre of an assault by Soviet tanks. Fourteen unarmed Lithuanians were killed on that evening, and many more were injured. The event caused outrage internationally and became a turning point in the collapse of the Soviet regime. There is a memorial and photographic exhibition at the base of the tower that, for anyone with an interest in or any respect for the history of Lithuania, is well worth a visit and a few moments of stoic silence.

ⓐ Sausio 13-osios 10 ⓣ +370 5252 5333 ⓦ www.lrtc.lt ⓗ 10.00–21.00

**Žaliasis Tiltas**

The Green Bridge boasts four statues that are the only remaining communist propaganda erections in Vilnius, constructed in the stern proud style of socialist realism. The four statues represent agriculture (sculptors B Bučas and P Vaivada), industry (N Petrulis and B Vyšniauskas), peace (B Pundzius) and youth (J Mikėnas and J Kėdainis). It's easy to look at them with a wry smile today, and, given that they haven't been blown up, decapitated or even defaced, one can only assume that the locals that lived under communism have learned to do just that. The first bridge to span the Neris was built here in 1536, and boasted a roof and shops. It has been damaged or destroyed and rebuilt several times, most recently in 1952.

*A tribute to the esteemed Mr Zappa*

## CULTURE

### Russian Drama Theatre

Despite the name, this is the venue for a wide variety of theatrical performances, although not many (if any) are in English. Still, it's an 'experience' as it's a bit of an old-style theatre with awkward seating that, if it weren't for the fact that only about twelve people turn up for each performance, would give you a great view of the back of someone else's head. There's a sense of easy-going culture about the place, as students often turn up, slouch themselves across three seats, and read a book while waiting for a performance to begin. In some ways, it can feel a bit more honest and genuine than some slick and modern theatre experience.
ⓐ Basanavičiaus 13 ⓣ +370 5262 7133

## RETAIL THERAPY

### Akropolis

A large shopping centre with a wide range of fashion and food shops, as well as one of the best bookstores in all of Lithuania (even if it only has one shelf of English-language books). Akropolis is not just a Mecca for shoppers, but also a good hub of entertainment, with cinemas and an ice-skating rink thoughtfully placed in the middle of it all. ⓐ Ozo 25 ⓣ +370 5248 4848 ⓦ www.akropolis.lt
🕒 08.00–24.00

### Europa

This small and modern shopping centre, occupying the lower floors of a shiny elliptical tower, offers mostly fashion stores, a few restaurants, and a supermarket. On the second floor, there are egg-shaped pods protruding from the balcony and offering an interesting seating location for some of the cafés. ⓐ Konstitucijos 7a ⓣ +370 5248 7070 ⓛ Shops 10.00–22.00, restaurants 08.00–24.00

**Kalvarių Market**

While Vilnius is striving to be all shiny and new, and isn't doing a bad job of it, it's nice to know this place still offers a more old-fashioned and authentic experience. It's a huge outdoor expanse sprawling with stalls and swarming with bargain hunters. Hours can be spent simply wandering around enjoying the hustle and bustle of it all, but keep in mind that some of the goods you purchase might not last that long. ⓐ Kalvarijų 61 ⓛ From before you'll want to go there until lunchtime

## TAKING A BREAK

**Fortas £** ❶ Cleverly divided into different areas for different styles of dining, you can come here to sit at the bar, slump into a sofa, pretend you're in a diner, or sit at a table that appears to be in someone's living room. ⓐ Algirdo 17 ⓣ +370 5265 2526 ⓛ 08.00–24.00 Mon–Thur, 11.00–24.00 Sat, 12.00–24.00 Sun

**Romano Gary £** ❷ One of those somewhat hidden treasures, this café has a very relaxed intellectual style about it, and is the perfect place to settle in with a book and hide away from the maddening crowd. The food might not warrant a Michelin star, but is a notch above standard café fare, and reasonably priced. To add to their alternative-intellectual air, they play Radio Užupis. ⓐ Basanavičiaus 16/5 ⓣ +370 5265 1950 ⓛ 09.00–22.00 Mon–Thur, 09.00–23.00 Fri, 11.00–23.00 Sat, closed Sun

**Vingio Park** ❸ The enormous park could occupy you for hours, if you don't mind walking around untended nature. In the middle is a huge arena – a monstrous half-bowl of benches overlooking a large cleared area which is often used for concerts. There's also a reasonable café-cum-restaurant behind the arena, with a little area for kiddies to play.

## AFTER DARK

### Bars & clubs

**Galaxy** Most notable as being the biggest club space in town, as capable of consuming a thousand people and turning them into a sweaty swarm as it is of attracting decent foreign DJs and other acts. Other than bigness, however, there's nothing special about the place – it could be Big Club, Anywhere – and therefore is probably only worth a visit if you are in town long enough to get sick of clubs that look like barnyards or caves. ⓐ Konstitucijos 26 ⓣ +370 5263 6666 ⓛ 22.00–06.00 Fri & Sat

**Gravity** It was a bomb shelter in days gone by, and you'll still enjoy the novelty of entering through a long concrete tunnel. It was also a great club in days gone by, but some kind of lazy arrogance seems to have crept in and they're still strafing crowds with unspectacular lighting in a grimy and dated interior while many other clubs have all sorts of new tricks to offer. The music is very good, and international DJs are often billed, but the place still feels a bit stale. ⓐ Jasinskio 16 ⓣ +370 5249 7966 ⓦ www.clubgravity.lt ⓛ 22.00–05.00 Fri & Sat

**Men's Factory** Despite being Vilnius's only gay club, you don't have to be gay to go there. Indeed, considering the work that has gone into fitting the place out with fun phallic furniture and iron cobwebs, it would be a shame not to go there just to see it. Still, the testosterone brigade stays away in droves, which makes the club popular with local girls who want to have fun without being hit on. The music tends to be of the heavy-rhythm techno kind that encourages something more like stomping than dancing. There's lots of suspiciously private rooms tucked away down lots of mysterious staircases, so you can probably get as devious as you want to, but if you stay in the open and have a bit of an open mind, you'll have good clean fun. We should mention, however, that security is very tight. You will have to pass through an airport-style metal detector and hand over any mobile phone that has a built-in camera before they will let you in. ⓐ Ševčenkos 16 ⓣ +370 6998 5009 ⓦ www.gayclub.lt ⓛ 22.00–04.00 Wed & Thur, 22.00–07.00 Fri & Sat

*The right bank of the River Neris at night*

**Sky Bar** The cocktail bar perched atop the Reval Hotel offers stunning views of Vilnius Old Town. The people who come here can also be quite a sight as they tend to dress to impress, so you won't know which way to look. Of course, the prices are also sky high, but you didn't come here for a bargain, so you probably won't mind just this once. Or twice. ⓐ Konstitucijos 20 (Reval Hotel Lietuva) ⓣ +370 5272 6272 ⓦ www.revalhotels.com ◷ 16.00–01.00, until 02.30 Fri & Sat

**Velvet** This place has little more than curiosity value. It's like a disco on the top deck of a bus, with all manner of sportswear, cheap jewellery and dim bimbos hanging off blokes who think they're the hottest thing going. Of course they'll take any opportunity to remind themselves of how 'big time' they are, and as such, it would not be wise to go here alone. Besides, if you go with a friend you can both have a good laugh. ⓐ Mykolaičio Putino 5 ⓣ +370 5231 2118 ◷ 21.00–05.00

◗ *Druskininkai's Russian Orthodox church*

OUT OF TOWN
trips

# Trakai

If you've been shopping for postcards or coffee-table books full of pretty pictures of Lithuania, Trakai will need no introduction. It's the place with the gorgeous castle plonked on an island in the middle of a lovely lake. It looks like something out of a fairy tale. While there is more to Trakai than the castle, which is a bit more modest than it appears in all the pictures, there is no doubt that it is the central attraction, and one you can't go past.

Trakai is about 25 km from Vilnius, and can easily be visited in half a day. Most hotels will either offer a shuttle bus, or can make arrangements with tour companies that offer them. While their services may be very convenient, they're not cheap.

Buses to Trakai depart from the Vilnius Bus Station every half an hour or so, and will deposit you at the not very conveniently located Trakai Bus Station. Or 'Bus Shack'. Once you get off the bus, you need to keep walking in the same direction that the bus was heading. Follow the road for about 1.5 km and you'll come across the castle.

## SIGHTS & ATTRACTIONS

### Trakai Castle

Trakai Castle dates from sometime in the 14th century, but was almost completely destroyed during times of conflict with the Russians during the 17th and 18th centuries. Restoration has been a stop-start affair since 1905. Imperial Russian authorities commenced reconstruction but things got interrupted by a couple of wars before the Soviets decided that rebuilding the castle would be an inappropriate celebration of Lithuania's feudal past (or something) and brought a halt to the whole thing again. Most

Vilnius Region
0
25km
50km
0
15 miles
30 miles
City
Large Town
Small Town
Motorway
Main Road
Minor Road
Airport
Railway
Estonia
Vilnius Region
Belarus
Poland
Ukraine
Baltic Sea
Courland Lagoon
LITHUANIA
RUSSIAN FEDERATION
POLAND
BELARUS
VILNIUS
Vilnius
Klaipėda
Šeduva
Panevėžys
Kelmė
Anykščiai
Utena
Šilutė
Raseiniai
Tauragė
Kėdainiai
Ukmergė
Molėtai
Jurbarkas
Jonava
Neman
Neris
Kaunas
Kaišiadorys
Elektrėnai
Trakai
Vilkaviškis
Prienai
Marijampolė
Alytus
Nemunas
Šalčininkai
Varėna
Druskininkai
294
Juozapinės Kalnas
A12
A1
A2
A6
A8
A11
A216
A229
A16
A3
A5
A15
A4
M7
M11
P45

recent restoration took place in the '80s and '90s, so what you're seeing when you look at the castle now is actually pretty fresh. Don't let that dilute the magic, however – it still looks very medieval and is even used occasionally as a location for period drama involving kings and queens and knights in shining armour.

There is a museum inside the castle, which is worth a visit, but just walking around the outside is also a pleasure if you prefer to spend your money renting a sailing boat (available, with someone who knows the ropes, from the bridge that you have to go over to reach the castle).

ⓐ Pilies Island ⓣ +370 5285 8246

## CULTURE

### Karaite Ethnographic Museum

Some will say they were 'invited' while others will say they were 'enslaved', but whichever way you look at it, a group of Karaite people from Crimea (Mesopotamia – modern-day Iraq) came to Trakai in the 15th century to act as bodyguards for Lithuania's Grand Duke Vytautas. A small community of these people still live in Trakai today, and have maintained their customs, culture and language. You can eat their food, look at their little coloured wooden houses (each of which has only three windows – one for God, one for the family and one for the Grand Duke), and sometimes see them standing by their front gates in traditional dress selling trinkets. If you fancy more than a cursory glance at

*Preparing to sail past Trakai Castle*

this fascinating community, however, a visit to this museum is a must.

Ⓐ Karaimų 22 Ⓣ +370 5285 5286

## RETAIL THERAPY

As Trakai becomes a bit of a tourist circus in summer, stalls pop up around the shore of the lake selling cheap sunglasses, jewellery, hot dogs, amber, ice creams and all manner of souvenirs. Of all those items, the hot dogs will probably prove to be the most durable. It's actually a bit of a credit to the community at Trakai that no more intrusive and permanent gift shops have blighted the pleasant little village. After all, you didn't come here to go shopping, did you?

## TAKING A BREAK

There are a few restaurants dotted along the shore facing the castle, and we've listed those below. However, don't overlook the self-catering and picnic options. Why not eat your lunch and sip some bubbly on a gently drifting boat? Or just wander off to one of the less populated but equally pretty banks of the lake to enjoy the view without being within earshot of the old man who stands on the bridge playing the *Chicken Dance* on his accordion every time someone wanders by.

**Kibininė £** While this place has a bit less to offer in terms of atmosphere, it is probably the best choice for trying *kibinai*, the Karaite traditional dish that can be found here, and featured in a

*Beautiful buildings are everywhere!*

30-second film used to fill the gaps between programmes on the Discovery Channel. *Kibinai* are essentially pastry pockets full of spicy and juicy meat and onions. ⓐ Karaimų 65 ⓣ +370 5285 5865

**Kybyniar** £ This is a lovely little cottage, tastefully decorated to offer a homely but not at all unsophisticated spot for lunch. Unfortunately, however, it doesn't offer a view of the castle at all. What it does offer is a menu of meals that are above par for such a touristy area, including *kibinai*. ⓐ Karaimų 29 ⓣ +370 5285 5179

## AFTER DARK

If you don't fancy going to one of the restaurants listed below, then when the sun goes away, so should you. There's nothing interesting in Trakai as far as nightlife goes. Watching the sun set over the castle is awesome, as is spending a few moments looking at the castle all nicely lit up after dark, but after that there's no reason to hang around. The only exception to this would be the occasional rave-style party events – there's generally one every summer.

**Apvalaus Stalo Klubas** ££ The name translates to the 'round table club', but they could also have justifiably called it 'best view of the castle'. The vista here is wonderful, as you can look out across the lake toward the castle, and have your view interrupted only by people taking photographs. They have taken advantage of the spot by creating two different restaurants in the one venue. Upstairs is the proper restaurant, where you get fine linen, chairs wearing dresses, and the best view of the castle to enjoy as you dine on

*Pretty houses in a Trakai side street*

French food. Downstairs is the 'pizzeria' restaurant, which is a bit more casual and, despite the name, offers a range of meals. In addition, there are plenty of places to sit outdoors (weather permitting, of course) and even a pontoon for meals afloat. Keep in mind that the castle is lit in the evenings, so even an after-dark meal here offers wonderful views. ⓐ Karaimų 53a ⓣ +370 5285 5595 ⓦ www.asklubas.lt

**Csarda ££** This is one of the newer restaurants in Trakai, and as it doesn't have a view and isn't in the sort of location where tourists with empty stomachs and full wallets might easily stumble across it, it has to rely on good food and a good reputation to draw the crowds. The food is Hungarian and is both hearty and tasty. There's also Hungarian wine and vodka available. If you're not hungry for Hungarian, however, there are also plenty of international and Lithuanian-style meals on the menu. If you're staying in Trakai for more than a day or two, and have had your fill of castle views, this is well worth the short taxi ride. ⓐ Aukštadvario 28a ⓣ +370 6165 5366

*Trakai Castle dates from the 14th century*

# Druskininkai

This is Lithuania's spa-resort town, famed for its salty spring waters. The word Druskininkai is formed from the Lithuanian word for salt (*druska*), and the whole town was formed around the salty springs. They also specialise in mud, hot rocks, beating you with bits of hot, wet trees and other earthy forms of therapy and pampering. In just the last few years, Druskininkai has been rapidly growing in popularity and earning quite a reputation not just for the health resorts, but also for active holidays and naughty weekends. In 2003, *Newsweek* magazine hailed it as being among Europe's top-ten health resorts. Even since then, new hotels have been popping up, and the standard of service and accommodation has been steadily increasing. And yet there are still options to stay in a shack by a stream where the goats will try to eat your luggage and the owners communicate in grunts – if that's what you want. Druskininkai successfully combines a basic and natural kind of appeal with as many, or as few, modern luxuries and conveniences as you may wish. For location, see map on page 101.

## GETTING THERE

There are a few buses each day from Vilnius Bus Station to Druskininkai. Keep in mind that some buses headed for Warsaw will pass through Druskininkai, adding to the options. Buses to Druskininkai leave more frequently from Kaunas than from Vilnius, so if you're planning to drop in on Kaunas, it might be a good idea to get a bus from there – but the total journey time would probably be more than four hours.

*Lake Druskonis is a peaceful spot*

If you're driving, follow signs first to Kaunas, and then take the turn-off to Trakai. After that, there are signs that lead you along the 130 km or so to Druskininkai.

Journey time will be about two hours in a bus, and about an hour and a half in a car.

## SIGHTS & ATTRACTIONS

### Architecture

While parts of Druskininkai are looking all shiny and new and fresh from the developer, there is still plenty of weird '60s-style, out-there architecture to make wandering around town well worthwhile. For some reason, health resorts in the Soviet era were all made to look like concrete fossils of space ships, as you will notice if you stroll around the building at Vilniaus 11. Contrasting this is the scattering of little wooden buildings, often in flaking coloured paint.

### Gruto Parkas – Soviet statue park

This is, without a doubt, the single must-see attraction anywhere near Druskininkai. Indeed, 'Stalinworld' is worthy of a place at the top of the list for any visitor to Lithuania, whether they intend to come to Druskininkai or not. Many people visit Gruto as a day-trip from Vilnius.

Quite simply, Gruto is a Soviet statue theme park. Many of the statues of Lenin and a small selection of the Stalins that were scattered around Lithuania have ended up here. However, what is most interesting at Gruto Parkas is not the towering commie carcasses themselves, but the theme-park presentation of them, and the merrily mocking way the locals interact with them.

*Communist statues in Gruto Parkas tell a story*

In what can seem a curious turnaround, people who would once have shuffled grudgingly past these statues now turn up to pull faces at them, pose for photos alongside them, or just point and laugh. Such behaviour is, of course, not without controversy, but it seems that many Lithuanians have concocted a recipe for dealing with a miserable past that contains more humour than aimless hatred. It's something that those of us who have never been subjected to live under the Soviet regime can't really claim to understand. But we can watch.

The statues are arranged along a path, and do not enjoy the protection of a little fence. You can go and stand beside them, put your handbag on their heads, pretend to be wiping their noses or ramming an umbrella into their ears and generally muck around.

Most of the statues and busts are accompanied by a small panel with a photo and description of the original location. In the case of the huge statue of Lenin that stood in Lukiškių Aikštė, the 'red square' on Gedimino that now has a big empty space in the middle, there is a dramatic photo of the statue being knocked down. You can also see one of only three statues ever made of Lenin having a well-earned sit down.

Also dotted along the path are guard towers that make a mockery of a concentration camp, and speakers cranking out cheesy Soviet propaganda music. Oh – and much of the park is set around small lakes or big puddles of the type favoured by big mosquitoes that could probably suck the blood out of the statues if they tried, but will prefer to eat you instead. It all adds up to quite a strange experience.

To get to Gruto Parkas, just mention the park to the driver of any bus that is going between Vilnius and Druskininkai, and he will be happy to show you where to disembark. From the bus stop, it's

◐ *The park is full of imposing statues*

about a 1-km walk down the side road to the park – a sign points you in the right direction.
Ⓣ +370 3135 5511 Ⓦ www.grutoparkas.lt

## CULTURE

### Forest Echo Museum

If it's made out of wood and serves no possible purpose, you'll probably find it somewhere in this big wooden shack that somehow seems to be floating among the trees by the side of the road. There are actually very many beautiful wooden creations scattered all about Lithuania – bus stops shaped like mushrooms, pagan 'totem' poles, big wooden crosses, children's play equipment shaped like animals – but if you don't have the time or the inclination for the random wanderings that would lead you to them, you can get a pretty good idea of the sorts of things that can be done with wood here. Don't forget to make a call on the wooden telephone while you're here.
Ⓐ M K Ciurlionio 116 Ⓣ +370 3135 3901 Ⓦ www.dmu.lt

## TAKING A BREAK

If you're in Druskininkai, you're already taking a break. There's no other reason to be there. When you need to take a break from your break, however, we suggest any of the following:

**Regina £** A very pleasant hotel restaurant, ideal for an evening meal with either good company or a good book, but otherwise a bit dull.
Ⓐ T Koscuškos 3 Ⓣ +370 3135 9060 Ⓦ www.regina.lt

◀ *A café in Druskininkai with a rustic setting*

**Sicilia £** While this is essentially a pizza joint, the two locations both offer atmosphere and edible options that make it a nice casual change from the hotel restaurant or satisfying change from the backpacker bread roll and cheese. Both locations – which are actually just a short pizza fling away from each other – offer a pleasant garden setting, and one is by a river. ⓐ Taikos 9 ⓐ Čiurlionio 56 ⓦ www.sicilia.lt

## AFTER DARK

**Dangaus Skliautas £** Druskininkai has a way of sprinkling everything with strangeness in the same way that fast-food restaurants sprinkle everything with salt. This place is certainly no exception. It's a low-key restaurant most evenings, but can become interesting at the weekend when they attempt to become a nightclub, and you consume too much beer and then attempt to say the name of the place to everyone you see. Or get tangled in the boudoir curtains that strangely dangle about some of the dining booths. ⓐ Kurorto 8 ⓣ +370 3135 1819

**Kolonada £** This music club and restaurant was first established in 1928, and still has an air of elegance and charm that seems somehow to stem from that era – although that doesn't mean you have to wear a shapeless dress with a too-low waist, a hat like a teapot atop polished short hair and smoke with a long cigarette holder. The club was cleaned up and reopened in 2004 and has been attracting a good range of jazz, blues, rock 'n' roll and classic performances. Weekends are the best time to go, as the weeknights tend only to offer the performances of a DVD player. ⓐ Kudirkos 22 ⓣ +370 3135 1222 ⓦ www.kolonada.lt

## ACCOMMODATION

**Regina** ££ They've got the balance of uncomplicated comfort just right here – it's pleasant enough for a weekend away with someone special, while also affordable. They also do some very attractive package deals that include the use of the health resort and spa facilities. ⓐ Kosciuškos 3 ⓣ +370 3135 9060 ⓦ www.regina.lt

**Vilnius Spa** ££ It looks a bit like something that just fell to earth from Andromeda, and that's just from the outside. This is the place to come for a 'trip' into health land, where they can not only put you up for the night, but smother you in mud, massage you with rocks, and so on. ⓐ Dineikos 1 ⓣ +370 3135 9160 ⓦ www.spa-vilnius.lt

**Europa Royale** ££–£££ A renovated 18th-century manor is now home to one of the swishest hotels in town, with rooms that come complete with an abundance of luxury. ⓐ Vilniaus 7 ⓣ +370 5266 0777 ⓦ www.europaroyale.com

# Klaipėda

Lithuania's coastal region centres around the seaport of Klaipėda – the former Prussian city of Memel. It's a long way from Vilnius – 300 km as the crow flies, and nearly four hours on a bus, five on the train – but worthwhile if you are spending any more than a short time in Lithuania. Especially, but not only, in summer.

From Klaipėda you can easily go to the Curonian Spit or Palanga, two vastly different options that would appeal to different tastes.

The Curonian Spit is a long finger of land that pokes out from Kaliningrad into the Baltic Sea and comes 'that close' to touching Klaipėda at its tip. The top half of the spit is Lithuanian territory, while the bottom half is Russian. The entire Curonian Spit is an area of unique and beautiful nature, and tends to be very tranquil even in summer.

Palanga is a pretty straightforward beach-and-party town in summer, and a popular destination for the easily amused. In off-peak seasons, it is a pleasant and quiet village in a lovely seaside location, but it is crowded, raucous and a bit plastic-fantastic in summer. For location, see map 101.

## GETTING THERE

Buses leave from Vilnius Bus Station to Klaipėda at 06.00, 07.00, 08.50 and 14.50. There are other buses that wiggle their way through a string of small villages on the way, but that drags the journey time out to something like six hours, so it's not recommended unless you like looking at lots of dusty little villages.

◐ *A constant military presence in Klaipėda*

Trains are also available to whisk you across Lithuania to Klaipėda. You can check the latest schedules on the Lithuanian Railways website, but be aware that the English version of the website seems not to list all trains, and the Lithuanian version is actually quite easy to use if you just choose the 'from' (*iš*) and 'to' (*į*) stations from the drop-down menu Ⓦ www.litrail.lt. The pleasantness or otherwise of the train journey will depend very much on who you share a cabin with. Seat allocations that are printed on the tickets tend to be ignored.

One advantage of travelling to Klaipėda on the earlier train is that it will stop in Šiauliai at about 09.20. This is home to the famed Hill of Crosses, and you can easily get off the train in Šiauliai, visit the hill, spend some time exploring Šiauliai itself, and then continue on to Klaipėda. Trains from Šiauliai to Klaipėda that are convenient for this purpose leave at 17.10 (arriving at 20.08) and 19.40 (arriving at 21.44). We don't have space to cover Šiauliai in detail here, but there's plenty of detail about it on the *In Your Pocket* website Ⓦ www.inyourpocket.com. The Šiauliai Tourist Information Centre will also be able to help in planning a visit, including making arrangements for a taxi to the Hill of Crosses Ⓦ www.siauliai.lt/tic Ⓣ +370 4152 3110

**Getting to the Curonian Spit from Klaipėda**

Many of the attractions and distractions we mention here are not in Klaipėda itself, but on the Curonian Spit. A car and passenger ferry shuffles to and from the spit on a pretty much non-stop basis, although you should check the last return time before you set out, to make sure you don't end up stranded. You should not count on getting back much later than 23.00 in summer. The ferry costs 1.50Lt for an adult passenger from Klaipėda to the Curonian Spit, but the

return journey is free. Getting a car across costs 32Lt which includes the driver, but passengers in the car must buy passenger tickets for the ferry. At the point where the ferry arrives on the Curonian Spit (called Smiltynė), there will be various buses and taxis offering to take you down the spit to Juodkrantė and Nida, the two main destinations along the way.
ⓐ Zvejų 8 ⓦ www.keltas.lt ⓣ +370 4631 1117

## SIGHTS & ATTRACTIONS

### Castle Museum

We can't tell you exactly what this place will be like because it's in the port area – a district that is changing so fast that every time we go there we end up lost and confused, walking around in circles without knowing it, but having a nice time anyway. Last time we checked, the museum was kind of half-done, but looked promising. Most of the museum is hidden under a grassy mound, and as such is not much to look at from the outside, but much more interesting inside, where you can see objects related to the history of the region in the 16th–18th centuries. Outside, excavation was taking place, revealing some of the original foundations of the fort. It's possible to wander around and get a sense of history being dug up before your very eyes. You can impress other tourists by putting sand in your hair and walking around with a little trowel and a brush, and a satisfied I've-just-unearthed-history kind of look on your face.

### The Simon Dach Fountain

The German poet Simon Dach (1605–51) is commemorated by a fountain that contains a statue of Aennchen von Tharsus. She was

the subject of an East Prussian lovesong that was once thought to have been composed by Dach. The sculpture was originally crafted by Berlin sculptor Alfred Kune. His version was erected in 1912, but disappeared sometime during World War II and was never heard of again. The version you see now was recreated in 1989 based on old photos.
ⓐ Teatro Aikštė

**Nida Dunes**
If it were not covered in all those hand-planted pine trees, the whole Curonian Spit would just blow away. As such, there are not too many parts of it that are not wooded, but you can still see the beautiful naked dunes just south of Nida. It's well worth exploring the area as it gives you not just stunning views, but a good sense of just how fragile the whole area is. You must, however, stick to the paths – there are plenty of them, so that's not going to be a problem. Randomly following the network of paths and heading in a general upward direction, you'll come across an old sundial.

This broken obelisk sticking out of an arrangement of various tiles was smashed to bits by a hurricane not long ago, but you can still see the engravings of runes that conjure up images of ancient tribes and fires tended by virgins and other such nonsense which is actually completely fanciful as the sundial is a contemporary creation.

Looking south from the sundial you are actually looking into Russia. If you've got good eyes, a good zoom lens or binoculars, you will be able to make out a line of black flags sticking out of the

*Klaipėda's very own guard dog!*

dunes. These mark the borders. If you fancy yourself as a bit of a spy, you can stand there monitoring the activities of sand dunes in Russia. And just think – there's probably someone down there looking back.

**Sea Museum**

A short walk to the right once you disembark the ferry will take you to the Sea Museum, which consists of some outdoor attractions (old boats, old shacks) that you will probably walk straight past to get to the big crowd pleaser – the aquarium. Housed in a strange building that was once a defence fort you will find all manner of fishy things to feast your eyes on. The interior of the building itself is also fun because it's not hard to imagine a James Bond villain moving in and filling all the pools with hungry sharks, ravenous piranha, electric eels, invisible deadly jellyfish, and so on.

Even more fun, especially if you have kiddies to keep amused, are the shows in which dolphins and sea lions put on all sorts of performances.

**Witches' Hill**

This is where three important Lithuanian traditions come together: wood carving, being a bit pagan, and being a bit crazy. The result is Witches' Hill (*Raganų Kalnas*) – a path that leads over the wooded dunes and is dotted along the way with various strange carved characters that variously have enormous tongues, wild hair, big bulging eyes and all manner of other strange features. With the wind whispering through the pines, shadows

*A Soviet Realist monument in Klaipėda*

flitting across the sandy path, and such goggle-eyed ghouls looking at you, it can verge on being a bit creepy – until you come across the two old blokes who crank up their accordions and sing badly in the hope that you will give them some money to make them shut up.

All the statues here were created by local artists, and the collection started coming together in 1980, and has grown over the past quarter of a century to become one of the main tourist attractions on the Curonian Spit.

## CULTURE

We can't really recommend a particular theatre or venue in Klaipėda for culture, but as you'll most probably be visiting in summer, you will tend to find the culture has a way of finding you. Temporary stages tend to pop up in outdoor spaces, including the big apron at the back of the Klaipėda Hotel, and the green triangle of land at the intersection of Tomo and Mėsininkų. You might also come across the performances in the grassy area by the lagoon shore in Juodkrantė.

The biggest cultural event of the year is the Klaipėda Sea Festival, held in summer each year, generally towards the end of July. For three days the city streets flood with people enjoying concerts, all manner of outdoor eating and drinking venues, stalls, markets, performances and more. If you do want to visit during the Sea Festival, be sure to book accommodation well in advance. Check the website for exact dates and a programme of events.
ⓦ www.svente.lt
There is also a jazz festival early in June ⓦ www.jazz.lt

## RETAIL THERAPY

There is certainly no unique shopping experience to be had in or around Klaipėda, but if you have kids to keep amused or suddenly have the desire to walk around looking at stuff that you might or might not buy and can see everywhere else anyway, then we recommend the following shopping centres.

### Akropolis

Just like the one in Vilnius, but maybe not so big. They also have cinemas and an ice-skating rink here, both of which are well worth keeping in mind as being a pleasant break from being all hot and sticky in summer. ⓐ Taikos 61 ⓦ www.akropolis.lt

### Big

Their claim that they are the biggest shopping centre is a bit dubious, but they are big and full of the same shops you find in other big, or even not so big, shopping centres. ⓐ Taikos 139 ⓣ +370 4636 0773 ⓦ www.big-klaipeda.lt

### MegaPlaza

If you're staying in central Klaipėda, this is the only shopping centre within walking distance. It's got shops. Other than that, there's not much to recommend it. It's certainly not mega. There's a dozen or so fashion shops and other familiar but forgettable outlets.
ⓐ H. Manto 21 ⓦ www.megaplaza.lt

## TAKING A BREAK

**Boogie Woogie £** This place might be considered a bit mediocre were it not in such a good location, but it attracts plenty of passing traffic and churns out cheap and cheery meals to keep them happy. ⓐ H Manto 5 ⓣ +370 4641 1844

**Čili Kaimas £** Tucked under a hideous concrete box – a former cinema, in fact – is Klaipėda's very own Čili Kaimas restaurant. The recipe here is exactly the same as that used to ensure success in Vilnius: good service, cheap but good-quality food, and oodles of calories. ⓐ H Manto 11 ⓣ +370 4631 0953 ⓦ www.cili.lt

**Senoji Hansa £** This small chain of otherwise un-noteworthy cafés has one location right near the main square in Old Town, and is therefore well worth seeking out. In summer, a canopy covers an outdoor seating area which always proves popular – so much so that they can, at times, struggle to provide good service. Food is both cheap and edible, but just relaxing with a drink and a snack seems to be the norm here. ⓐ Kurpių 1 ⓣ +370 4640 0056

**Navalis £–££** Spilling out from beneath one of the city's smartest hotels is an equally smart café where you can enjoy coffee, croissants, snacks and a spot of people-watching. ⓐ H Manto 23 ⓣ +370 4640 4200 ⓦ www.navalis.lt

*◀ Distinctive wooden architecture in Klaipėda*

**Ešerinė (Nida) ££** If you find yourself somewhere near Nida toward the end of the day, you could do a lot worse than take refuge beneath one of the island-style grass huts and order fish. The food is expensive here, but according to the rule of fin (that you get what you pay for) it is very nice, and enjoying delicious seafood with such a nice view across the lagoon is indeed a rare pleasure.
ⓐ Nagalių 2, Nida ⓣ +370 4695 2757

**Forto Dvaras ££** Another good option that has popped up in Klaipėda following success in Vilnius, this one being beneath the Klaipėda Hotel, overlooking a big patch of, erm, weeds. The wide variety of *cepelinai* is the main attraction here. ⓐ Naujoji Sodo 1 ⓣ +370 4630 0211 ⓦ www.fortopica.lt

**Pašiūrė (Nida) ££** At first appearance this may look like a grand restaurant, but it's actually a small seasonal affair and the outside seating that you see is all there is to it. Pop in to relax beside the tinkling fountain and be served by pretty young things in traditional Lithuanian dress bringing you traditional Lithuanian meals.
ⓐ Naglių 20, Nida ⓣ +370 6984 1538

## AFTER DARK

### Restaurants

**Memelis ££** An old warehouse facing the river has been turned into a fun-house for grown-ups, with a restaurant and beer hall downstairs, and a bar and nightclub upstairs. The menu offers piscatorial and Teutonic meals, in keeping with the traditions of the

*Ornate façade in Klaipėda*

region and the history of the building. However, it's a pretty basic and easy-going kind of place where big words would be frowned upon, so we can summarise that it's just fishy and German. There are pictures in the menu for those who can't read. They brew their own beer downstairs and are happy to serve it in ridiculous portions, such as in a tall four-litre glass tube with little taps at the bottom. You can set it up on the edge of the table, lie underneath it with your mouth open and ... we forget what happens after that. ⓐ Žvėjų 4 ⓣ +370 4640 3040 ⓦ www.memelis.lt

**Skandalas £££–£££** They couldn't cram more corny, American Route-66 kitsch in here if they tried. There are number plates and old advertisements and rock memorabilia all over the place. Oh – and a bronze Statue of Liberty looks out across it all. Also in a somewhat American style, meals are generous, simple and delicious, and the place gets hopping with a fun and friendly crowd at weekends. It's a bit of a stroll away from the centre, but well worth finding. ⓐ Kanto 44 ⓣ +370 4641 1585 ⓦ www.skandalas.info

**Bars & clubs**

**Eldorado** While you're not going to put this dive at the top of your list, it can be fun to drop in and see what's happening. It's the sort of place that can be really buzzing if the right crowd happens to have assembled there, but can also be a bit strange and grim. The good thing is that it is like a cellar hallway, with a stairway entrance at either end. You can go in one end, wander through to see what it's like, and make an easy escape at the other end if you don't like it. ⓐ Lietuvninkų 2 ⓣ +370 4642 1010

**Honolulu** There are a few nightclubs in Klaipėda, but to be honest, they are not always clean, safe or welcoming places. This is an exception. The over-21 door policy ensures giggly teens stay away and the steep entrance cost keeps the Shopswear-wearing skinheads sulking off to somewhere with lower standards and prices. The interior designers went coconuts with an island theme, but actually didn't have much room to play with and have left us with a club that is a bit cramped. ⓐ Naujoji Sodo 1 (underneath the Klaipėda Hotel) ⓣ +370 4640 4372 ⓦ www.klaipedahotel.lt

**Šikšnosparnio Lizdas (Bat's Nest)** Even the Goths are a bit weird in Lithuania. Actually, Goths are a bit weird everywhere, but they're *especially* weird in Lithuania, and they seem to have created a mildly creepy but fun spot here. There's a cave-like atmosphere, but lots of creative touches such as little 'windows' set into the table that display bits of old iron something-or-others. A fun place to settle in for the evening, although we're not sure we'd go there if there was a full moon. ⓐ Tiltų 5 ⓣ +370 4631 3412

**Live Music**

**Kurpiai** This is often touted as the best jazz club in Lithuania, and with good reason. Even when it hasn't attracted the hottest acts, it's a fun place to drop in and spend an evening. There is a wacky layout that makes the place feel that it was just chucked together, and the sort of atmosphere in which people who didn't arrive together end up dancing together. ⓐ Kurpių 1a ⓣ +370 4641 0555 ⓦ www.jazz.lt

## ACCOMMODATION

**Klaipėda Old Town Hostel** £ It's not actually in the Old Town, but it's right next to the bus station which is convenient for arrival and departure. While things are very basic here (just a couple of rooms crammed with bunks), it is a friendly and easy-going kind of place. The no-shoes policy makes it smell in summer. Take a peg. ⓐ Butkų Juzės 7–4 ⓣ + 370 4621 1879 ⓦ www.lithuanianhostels.org

**Astra** ££ It's a big white box on the outside, but very effeminate and fluffy on the inside, and ideally located right next to the ferry terminal, making it a great base for exploring both Klaipėda and the Curonian Spit. ⓐ Pilies 2 ⓣ +370 4631 3849 ⓔ hotelastra@takas.lt

**Klaipėda** ££ This landmark hotel (you can't miss it) shows what can be done with an old Soviet-style tower, a big bucket of money, and some fancy interior designers who know what to do with dark wooden panels, moody lighting and flat-screen televisions. If you can afford it, you won't regret it. ⓐ Naujoji Sodo 1 ⓣ +370 4640 4372 ⓦ www.klaipedahotel.lt

**Litinterp** ££ As is the case in Vilnius and Kaunas, Litinterp in Klaipėda offers simple, clean and comfortable accommodation at reasonable prices. The location is excellent given the price, but they can also organise home stays and accommodation in Nida and Palanga. ⓐ Puodžių 17 ⓣ +370 4641 0644 ⓦ www.litinterp.lt

*Higher Castle is an icon of Vilnius*

PRACTICAL
information

# Directory

## GETTING THERE

### By air

Lithuania is on the budget airline route – Ryanair flies to Kaunas (about 100 km from Vilnius) and British Airways, airBaltic and flyLAL (formerly Lithuanian Airlines) all flies between London Gatwick and Vilnius at reasonable prices. Polish airline WIZZ air also flies to Kaunas via Warsaw.

Many people are aware that air travel emits $CO_2$, which contributes to climate change. You may be interested in the possibility of lessening the environmental impact of your flight through the charity Climate Care, which offsets your $CO_2$ by funding environmental projects around the world. Visit climatecare.org

### By rail

Rail isn't always the best option for getting into and out of Lithuania, as trains tend to be slow and uncomfortable compared to buses. Rail is really only worth considering if you are coming from or going to Russia.

### By road

Regular buses ferry travellers between Vilnius and the other Baltic capitals, and are ideal for those who are also visiting Latvia and/or Estonia. Buses are also available to and from cities in Poland, and further west.

*Navigate your way around Vilnius*

ROTUŠĖ
TOWN HALL
AUŠROS VARTAI
GATES OF DAWN
VILNIAUS PAV
GALERIJA
VILNIUS
BASTĖJA
ARTILLERY BASTION
ŠV. DVASIOS BAŽNYČIA
CH. OF HOLY SPIRIT
TURIZMO INFORMACIJA
TOURIST INFORMATION
Belaidžio interneto zona
Wireless Internet zone

### By sea

Ferries travel to Klaipėda in Lithuania from Kiel and Sassnitz in Germany, Karlshamn in Sweden, and Århus (Aarhus), Åbenrå (Aabenraa) and Fredericia in Denmark.

## ENTRY FORMALITIES

Lithuania is a member of the EU and working towards becoming a member of the Schengen Zone, all of which has made many travelling restrictions melt away. Citizens of the EU, USA, Canada, Australia and New Zealand can turn up without a visa and stay for a given period of time – generally for a total of three months within any twelve – before having to worry about getting kicked out. Those who do require a visa will need to get health insurance. Exact details, including visa application procedures, are on the Lithuanian Ministry of Foreign Affairs website Ⓦ www.urm.lt

### Customs

EU citizens have no incoming customs restrictions, save those required for health and safety reasons, but cannot arrive with more then 10,000 litas in cash.

## TRAVEL INSURANCE

However you book your city break, it is important to take out adequate personal travel insurance for the trip. For peace of mind the policy should give cover for medical expenses, loss, theft, repatriation, personal liability and cancellation expenses. If you are travelling in your own vehicle you should also check that you are appropriately insured. Make sure you take relevant insurance documents and your driving licence with you.

Non-EU citizens may only bring one litre of spirits or two litres of wine or beer; and 200 cigarettes, or 100 cigarillos, 50 cigars or 250 g tobacco. Non EU-citizens are also limited to 50 g of perfume, or 250 ml of eau de toilette.

## MONEY

Lithuania was using the litas at the time of writing, but was hoping to adopt the euro at the start of 2007 – dependent on meeting certain economic requirements. The exchange rate was fixed at 3.45 litas to the euro in 2002. The rule of thumb for UK travellers is five litas to the pound.

ATMs are abundant in Vilnius – including at the airport, bus and train stations – but can be less common in smaller villages. Take plenty of cash if you are planning an out-of-town adventure.

Currency can be changed at bureaux de change at the airport and train stations, as well as many locations in the Old Town, including casinos – handy if you get stuck with a fist full of zloty, or something, late at night. Credit cards (MasterCard and Visa) are widely accepted.

## HEALTH, SAFETY & CRIME

Despite the fact that you can often see locals lugging around huge bottles of water, that which comes out of the taps is perfectly safe to drink. Vilnius is atop a big lump of permeable rock (an aquifer) that happily releases its water through various artesian wells to pumping and treatment stations. What you get out of the tap is basically spring water without the advertising.

The standard of public healthcare is very good, although the hospital facilities may not appear to be up to western standards, and a bribe system still persists. Private clinics abound and cater to a growing stream of health tourists from the UK who come here for operations, and of course the quality of service they provide is world-class. See the Emergencies section for more details.

Police in Lithuania, looking gruff and wearing green, are generally not helpful to tourists. They don't tell you the time or bid you good day or help old ladies (or anyone) to cross roads. They simply don't see that as part of their job. They should, however, be your first point of contact should you have trouble involving theft or, heaven forbid, violence. Don't mention the words 'lollipop' or 'cucumber' while in conversations with the police. When you see them, you'll know why.

The standard of personal safety is very high in Vilnius Old Town. Of course, you should exercise the usual caution to avoid becoming the victim of petty crime, but you're unlikely to be subject to a pickpocket pack-attack or broad-daylight mugging. Going out at night is generally safe, but stick to well-lit streets, stay in the Old Town, and don't do anything that makes you look like a gullible, vulnerable tourist.

Of course, there are some people who see foreigners as an easy target. As is the case anywhere, keep an eye on your drink. And, whatever you do, think long and hard about accepting an invitation to 'go back to my place' – it's probably not a good idea.

## OPENING HOURS

Opening hours can be a bit random, but standard business hours are from 09.00 to 18.00 for businesses, and from 12.00 to 24.00 for restaurants that don't serve breakfast.

*Vilnius government building*

Food stores (including supermarkets and mini-supermarkets) are generally open from 07.00 to 22.00 every day.

One thing to be aware of when planning your day is that while nightclubs might open at 22.00 or thereabouts, they are simply not worth going to until midnight. At weekends nightclubs close at about 05.00, and then many people simply head to one of the all-night cafés or bars. Vilnius is a city that doesn't encourage sleep.

Opening hours are usually printed on the doors of shops and restaurants, sometimes as a line of blocks or Roman numerals, one representing each day of the week. Monday is the first day of the week in Lithuania, and Sunday the last.

## TOILETS

The horrors of squatting have ceased. These days you'd have to go out of your way to find an old-fashioned Soviet-era toilet. Public toilets are available in a few parks and streets in the city, but probably not the ones where you happen to be when you need them. If you do find one, you'll have to pay to use it, but can expect a reasonable degree of cleanliness and safety. If there's not one nearby, the best option is to head into a café or hotel foyer and – if you have no intention of buying a coffee or becoming a customer – asking politely.

Be careful of the gender signs. The gents' is marked with a triangle which is broad at the top and pointed at the bottom (think 'broad shoulders') while the ladies' is marked with a triangle which is pointed at the top and broad at the bottom (think 'skirt'). You might also see 'V' for men (*vyrai*) and 'M' for women (*moterys*). The international 'WC' is used to signpost toilets.

*Higher Castle can easily be reached by funicular railway*

## CHILDREN

Children will be welcome in Vilnius as much as in any 'western' city. There are kiddy play areas in the parks, but you should be aware that the equipment in them is not as well maintained as you might like. There are no health-and-safety watchdogs here.

It's not common to find baby-change facilities in shops, cafés or restaurants, and high chairs are harder to come by than a big pile of hens' teeth. Nappies and other baby requirements are all available in supermarkets.

- **Akropolis** An ideal day out for older kids is a trip to the Akropolis shopping and entertainment centre – but not just because it's a shopping centre. It's also home of a handy ice-skating rink, as well as cinemas, plenty of restaurants, and – oh, yes – some shops. Keep in mind that if you go to the cinema, films are generally presented with original-language audio and Lithuanian subtitles, so not only will you get to see the latest Hollywood blockbuster, but you might learn the Lithuanian for 'hey', 'yo!' and 'big explosion, man'. (See page 94.)

- **Čili Kaimas** Downstairs, there's a large pool stocked with fish. Don't worry – they don't turn up on your dinner plate, but they do have a way of keeping kids amused, as do the live chickens near the entrance upstairs and the grass snake living in a big terrarium near the toilets. There's also a babushka – a Russian-style 'grandmother' who rattles out stories – and other theatrical entertainment for kids from 12.00 to 14.00 on

*Traditional dolls make attractive souvenirs for children*

Sundays. It's in Lithuanian only, but it might provide some distraction for the kids while you have a meal. Ⓐ Vokiecin 8 Ⓣ +370 5231 2536 Ⓛ 10.00–24.00 Sun–Thur, 10.00–02.00 Fri & Sat Ⓦ www.cili.lt

- **Marceliukės Klėtis** It's a taxi ride out of town, but this is one of the best restaurants to go to with children. Upstairs is a dining room surrounded by what can only be described as an adventure playground. There's a cubby house they can explore, lots of mysterious passageways and stairways, and a big slide made from what looks like a fallen log. There's even a big low table with little seats for little kids, in case they do actually want to sit down and eat. For family-friendly fun, this place is highly recommended, and it's also a decent place to try traditional Lithuanian food. Ⓐ Tuskulenu 3S Ⓣ +370 5272 5087 Ⓛ 11.00–24.00 Tues–Sat, 11.00–23.00 Mon & Sun

## COMMUNICATIONS

### Phones

Public telephones operate on a card system. You can pick up cards from post offices and Lietuvos Spauda kiosks. Paying for the call is the easy part. Working out Lithuania's baffling array of prefixes is the hurdle.

Basically, every phone number in Lithuania is prefixed with an 8 – but only if you're dialling from within Lithuania but not within the same city, and only if you're not using the international format. It's as if the whole country was covered by one area code.

A Vilnius telephone number has seven digits. The Vilnius city code, 5, plus the mystery '8' must be added to the front of those

*Europa Square represents the modern side of Vilnius*

Cipollino
monton

**CODES**

- The country code for Lithuania is 370. If you see a seven-digit Vilnius phone number, you can dial it by calling +370-5 followed by the number.
- To make an international call from within Lithuania, dial 00, and then the country code for the destination country, such as 44 for the UK, or 61 for Australia.
- For more information on the phone system, contact Lietuvos Telekomas. Call 117 from within Vilnius, or t +370 8000 0117 w www.telecom.lt

seven digits if you're calling from a mobile, or from anywhere outside of Vilnius.

### Post

The postal service is Lithuania is generally very good, although service can be rather abrupt in post offices, where you will inevitably have joined the wrong queue. The post office here, like those in the UK, deals with all sorts of non-postal matters such as bill payments, so a visit can be a bit tedious. You'll pay 1.70Lt to send a letter abroad from within Lithuania, and 1.20Lt to send a postcard. Instances of mail going missing are rare. See w www.post.lt for more detailed information.

### Internet

At the time of writing, most of Old Town was covered by free wi-fi internet, as were many of the good hotels. You can wander into most cafés and restaurants in the main tourist areas and expect to

*Shopping in Vilnius has changed dramatically since Soviet days*

be connected. The signal strength and connection speeds are both excellent. Lietuvos Telekomas, however, have been saying that the service would be free 'for now' – so we expect they will start charging for it anytime soon, but have no idea of what the rates will be or how they will be charged.

GPRS/3G/UMTS services were being introduced at the time of writing, and firm details were not available on access and pricing options for visitors. The mobile phone companies Bitė and Omnitel were both introducing 3G mobile services, so the best bet is to visit their shops (both on Gedimino, a short stroll from the Cathedral end).

If you don't have your own computer, you can get on the internet for free at the **British Council Library** (ⓐ 2nd floor, Jogailos 4 ◷ 10.00–18.00 Tues–Sat), or at **Mano Kavin**ė (ⓐ Bokšto) – where they will happily let you sip and surf, using the computer at the bar.

There is also an internet café called **Collegium** (ⓐ Pilies 22). The entrance isn't in the main street, so you have to go through the archway into the courtyard, and turn left, to find it. There are a few other computer salons scattered about, but they tend to be geared toward children who prefer to loudly kill each other as many times as possible, and as such are not well suited for tourists.

## ELECTRICITY

240 volts, 50 Hz AC. European-style two-pin sockets. Buy adaptors before you come – they're not readily available in the main tourist area. If you do need to buy an adaptor, head for the Akropolis shopping centre where you will find an 'Elektromarkt' store.

## TRAVELLERS WITH DISABILITIES

Things are improving rapidly – there are now plenty of wheelchair-friendly venues that are regrettably, impossible to get to. The cobbled streets, narrow pavements and abundance of stairs are still a problem for those with wheelchairs or mobility difficulties, but the city is making efforts to improve the situation.

The newer buses and trolleybuses now have friendly low-entry doors and space inside for wheelchairs. These are gradually replacing the older fleet of groaning and lumbering vehicles that had doors that made life difficult for wheelchair users.

**Lithuanian Council for Disabled Affairs** ⓦ www.lirt.lt

## TOURIST INFORMATION

Tourist information offices are located at:

ⓐ Vilniaus 22 ⓣ +370 5262 9660
ⓐ Didžioji 31 (Town Hall) ⓣ +370 5262 6470
ⓐ Geležinkelio 16 (Train Station) ⓣ +370 5269 2091
ⓦ www.turizmas.vilnius.lt

While their website cannot be relied upon to be up to date – it was still listing venues that had long since closed last time we checked – the staff at the Tourist Information Centres are generally multilingual, pleasant and helpful.

Those visiting Vilnius with an interest in Jewish history and culture should drop into the Jewish Community Centre ⓐ Pylimo 4 ⓣ +370 5261 3003

## FURTHER READING

*Vilnius In Your Pocket* is published every two months and maintains an up-to-date listing of hotels, pubs, clubs, restaurants, cafés and tourist attractions, all with independent reviews.

Tomas Venclova's book *Vilnius City Guide* provides an excellent overview of the city and its history, in a format that is small enough to stick in your bag and carry around as you explore.

## Useful phrases

Although English is widely spoken in Lithuania, these words and phrases may come in handy. See also the phrases for specific situations in other parts of the book.

| English | Lithuanian | *Approx. pronunciation* |
|---|---|---|
| | **BASICS** | |
| **Yes** | Taip | *Teip* |
| **No** | Ne | *Nya* |
| **Please** | Prašau | *Pra-show* |
| **Thank you** | Ačiū | *Ah-chyu* |
| **Hello** | Labas | *Lah-bahs* |
| **Goodbye** | Viso gero | *Vee-soh geh-roh* |
| **Excuse me/Sorry** | Atsiprašau | *Aht-see-prah-show* |
| **That's OK** | Viskas gerai | *Vees-kahs geh-ray* |
| **To** | Į | *Ee* |
| **From** | Iš | *Eesh* |
| **I don't speak Lithuanian** | Aš nekalbu lietuviškai | *Ash nya-kahl-boo lye-too-vish-kay* |
| **Do you speak English?** | Ar kalbate angliškai? | *Ahr kahl-bah-teh angle-ish-kay?* |
| **Good morning** | Labas rytas | *Lah-bas ree-tas* |
| **Good afternoon** | Laba diena | *La-bah dye-nah* |
| **Good evening** | Labas vakaras | *Lah-bas vah-car-us* |
| **Good night** | Labanakt | *Lah-bah-nuct* |
| **My name is ...** | Mano vardas ... | *Mano vahr-dahs ...* |
| | **DAYS & TIMES** | |
| **Monday** | Pirmadienis | *Peer-mah-dye-nees* |
| **Tuesday** | Antradienis | *Ant-rah-dye-nees* |
| **Wednesday** | Trečiadienis | *Trya-chya-dye-nees* |
| **Thursday** | Ketvirtadienis | *Kyat-veer-tah-dye-nees* |
| **Friday** | Penktadienis | *Penck-tah-dye-nees* |
| **Saturday** | Šeštadienis | *Shesh-tah-dye-nees* |
| **Sunday** | Sekmadienis | *Seck-mah-dye-nees* |
| **Morning** | Rytas | *Ree-tahs* |
| **Afternoon** | Popietė | *Popee-eh-teh* |
| **Evening** | Vakaras | *Wack-ahr-us* |
| **Night** | Naktis | *Nuck-tiss* |
| **Yesterday** | Vakar | *Vah-car* |

| English | Lithuanian | *Approx. pronunciation* |
| --- | --- | --- |
| **Today** | Šiandien | *Shyan-dyen* |
| **Tomorrow** | Rytoj | *Ree-toy* |
| **What time is it?** | Kelinta valanda? | *Kel-inn-tah vah-lan-dah?* |
| **It is ...** | Dabar ... | *Dah-bahr ...* |
| **09.00** | Devinta valanda | *Deh-veen-tah vah-lahn-dah* |
| **Midday** | Vidurdienis | *Wee-duhr-dye-niss* |
| **Midnight** | Vidurnaktis | *Wee-duhr-nackt-iss* |
| | **NUMBERS** | |
| **One** | Vienas | *Wienn-us* |
| **Two** | Du | *Doo* |
| **Three** | Trys | *Trees* |
| **Four** | Keturi | *Keh-too-ree* |
| **Five** | Penki | *Pyan-kee* |
| **Six** | Šeši | *Shya-shee* |
| **Seven** | Septyni | *Sep-tee-nee* |
| **Eight** | Aštuoni | *Ash-too-nee* |
| **Nine** | Devyni | *Deh-wee-nee* |
| **Ten** | Dešimt | *Dya-shimt* |
| **Eleven** | Vienuolika | *Wienn-oo-lick-ah* |
| **Twelve** | Dvylika | *Dwee-lick-ah* |
| **Twenty** | Dvidešimt | *Dwee-deh-shimt* |
| **Fifty** | Penkiasdešimt | *Penck-yas-dya-shimt* |
| **One hundred** | Šimtas | *Shim-tahs* |
| | **MONEY** | |
| **I would like to change these traveller's cheques/this currency** | Aš norėčiau iškeisti kelioninius čekius/šitą valiutą | *Ash-norr-etch-yau ish-case-tee kyal-on-in-oos check-oos/sheet-ah vah-loo-tah* |
| **Where is the nearest ATM?** | Kur artimiausias bankomatas? | *Kuhr ahr-tee-myau-syas bahn-koh-mah-tahs?* |
| **Do you accept traveller's cheques/credit cards?** | Ar priimate kelioninius čekius/kreditines korteles? | *Ur pre-eem-ut-teh cull-on-in-yus check-us/credit-iness cort-el-ess?* |
| | **SIGNS & NOTICES** | |
| **Airport** | Oro uostas | *Oh-roh ohs-tahs* |
| **Rail station** | Geležinkelio stotis | *Girl-ezh-ink-ello stoh-tiss* |
| **Platform** | Platforma | *Plat-form-ah* |
| **Smoking/ non-smoking** | Rūkoma/ nerūkoma | *Roo-koh-mah/ nya-roo-koh-mah* |
| **Toilets** | Tualetas | *Too-al-et-us* |
| **Ladies/Gentlemen** | Moterų/Vyrų | *Mot-err-oo/Weer-oo* |
| **Underground** | Metro | *Met-roh* |

# Emergencies

## EMERGENCY NUMBERS

**112** is the all-purpose emergency number. It works from any fixed or mobile phone in Lithuania. It should be used for genuine emergencies only – such as when you need police, an ambulance, or the fire brigade. Emergencies of the 'chocolate and flowers at midnight' variety are best dealt with by calling the general-information services 118 or 1588, for which you will pay a small fee.

## MEDICAL SERVICES

The main public hospital is the **Vilnius University Emergency Hospital** ⓐ Šiltnamių 29 ⓣ +370 5216 9140

There are several private hospitals with English-speaking staff that offer 24-hour emergency care. These include:

**Baltic American Medical & Surgical Clinic** ⓐ Nemenčinės 54a ⓣ +370 5234 2020

**Medical Diagnostic Centre** ⓐ V Grybo 32/10 ⓣ +370 5270 9120

For general medical help during business hours, the most central and convenient option is the **Med General Private Clinic** ⓐ Gedimino 1a/19, 2nd floor ⓣ +370 5261 3534

**Pharmacies** (*vaistinė*) are so plentiful as to be difficult to avoid.

For dental help, contact **Stomatologijos Klinika** ⓐ Labdarių 7/11 ⓣ +370 5261 9623

### Roadside help

**Altas Assistance** can turn up and get you going anywhere in Lithuania ⓣ +370 8001 8100 or 1810. In Vilnius, they have a 35Lt call-out fee, to which the costs of any work that needs to be done will be added. Out of town, expect to pay 75Lt for the call-out.

## CONSULATES & EMBASSIES

**Australia (consulate)** Ⓐ Vilniaus 23 Ⓣ +370 5212 3369
**Canada** Ⓐ Jogailos 4 Ⓣ +370 5249 0950
**Republic of Ireland** Ⓐ Jogailos 4 Ⓣ +370 5269 0044
**UK** Ⓐ Antakalnio 2 Ⓣ +370 5246 2900
**USA** Ⓐ Akmenų 6 Ⓣ +370 5266 5500
**New Zealand and South Africa** do not have representation in Lithuania.

### EMERGENCY PHRASES

**Help!** Padėkite! *Pah-deck-it-eh!* **Fire!** Gaisras! *Ghays-rus!*
**Stop!** Stop! *Stop!*

**Call an ambulance/a doctor/ the police/the fire brigade!**
Iškvieskite greitąją pagalbą/gydytoją/policiją/gaisrininkus!
*Ish-ques-kee-teh gray-tah-yah pah-gull-bah/ghee-dee-toh-yah/poh-lee-tsee-yah/ghay-sree-neen-coos!*

The publishers would like to thank the following for supplying the copyright photographs for this book: Lars Bryne 75; Druskininkai Tourist Information: page 111, 116; Klaipėda City Municipality: page 113; Pictures Colour Library: pages 40, 146; Andrew Quested: pages 15, 17, 19, 33, 34, 39, 42, 47, 49, 67, 71, 75, 85, 87, 103, 105, 106, 113, 127, 130, 139; Richard Schofield: pages 45, 99, 121, 124; Tourism Division of Vilnius City Municipal Government: pages 5, 7, 9, 12, 21, 23, 27, 31, 59, 61, 93, 97, 109, 115, 137, 143, 145, 149, 150.

Copy editor: Natasha Reed
Proofreader: Janet McCann

**Send your thoughts to**
## books@thomascook.com

- **Found a great bar, club, shop or must-see sight that we don't feature?**
- **Like to tip us off about any information that needs updating?**
- **Want to tell us what you love about this handy little guidebook and more importantly how we can make it even handier?**

Then here's your chance to tell all! Send us ideas, discoveries and recommendations today and then look out for your valuable input in the next edition of this title. As an extra 'thank you' from Thomas Cook Publishing, you'll be automatically entered into our exciting monthly prize draw.

Send an email to the above address (stating the book's title) or write to: CitySpots Project Editor, Thomas Cook Publishing, PO Box 227, The Thomas Cook Business Park, Unit 18, Coningsby Road, Peterborough PE3 8SB, UK.